Barna

SPIRITUAL CONVERSATIONS
IN THE
DIGITAL AGE

*How Christians' Approach to
Sharing Their Faith Has Changed in 25 Years*

A Barna Report
Produced in Partnership with
Lutheran Hour Ministries

Scripture quotations marked MSG are taken from *THE MESSAGE,* copyright © 1993, 1994, 1995, 1996, 2000, 2001, 2002 by Eugene H. Peterson. Used by permission of NavPress. All rights reserved. Represented by Tyndale House Publishers, Inc.

Scripture quotations marked (NLT) are taken from the Holy Bible, New Living Translation, copyright ©1996, 2004, 2015 by Tyndale House Foundation. Used by permission of Tyndale House Publishers, Inc., Carol Stream, Illinois 60188. All rights reserved.

CONTENTS

A MULTI-YEAR LOOK AT AMERICA'S FAITH

You are reading the first of three research reports from Barna, in partnership with Lutheran Hour Ministries. These studies seek to reveal how Americans are expressing their faith: from the conversations individuals have, to the influence of households on spiritual development, to the impact of Christians on the broader community. Join us as we discover both the private and the public ways faith continues to shape American life.

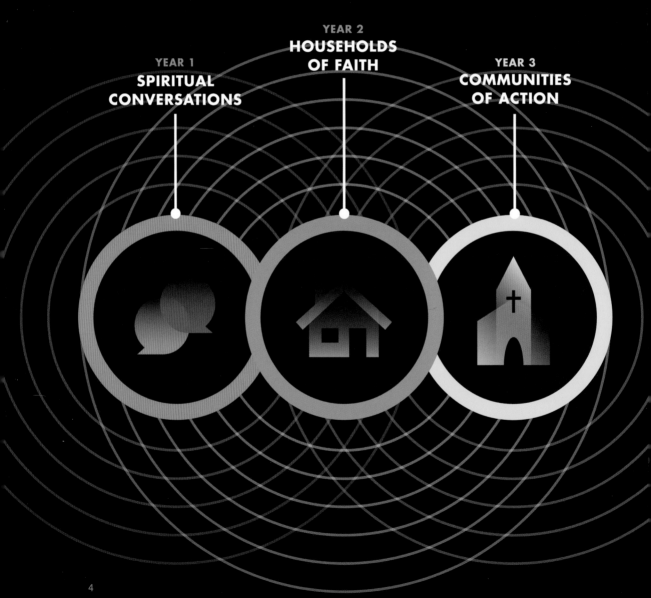

YEAR 1
SPIRITUAL CONVERSATIONS

YEAR 2
HOUSEHOLDS OF FAITH

YEAR 3
COMMUNITIES OF ACTION

PREFACE

BY KURT S. BUCHHOLZ

President & CEO of Lutheran Hour Ministries

In the Western world our congregations are shrinking.

It's a reality that's hard to deny when we sit in the pews on Sunday morning. Month by month, the list of fellow believers who have gone on to heaven continues to exceed the list of new believers baptized. When you look around on a given Sunday and see fewer and fewer people, it can be easy to panic.

Anecdotal evidence suggests that churchgoing families are having fewer children than previous generations—but that's not the only reason for the decline, and it's not the one that keeps me up at night. The more alarming problem is this: Fewer adults are being brought into a saving relationship with Jesus Christ. As the president of Lutheran Hour Ministries, a ministry that exists to empower and embolden lay people for outreach, I feel particular anxiety over that point. If adults aren't being brought into the Church, it stands to reason that our regular methods of evangelism simply aren't working like they once did. If something has changed in our culture, shouldn't our outreach strategies change, too? If Lutheran Hour Ministries exists to embolden God's people to share his love, what do we need to do differently?

These are big questions that require big answers. In 1993, we partnered with Barna to research reasons people did and did not engage in intentional outreach. That data is an excellent resource—but a lot has changed in our culture since that initial study, especially in the area of technology. Digital avenues have opened up to reach and engage more people than ever before, and at a fraction of the cost. But how can the Church best use these new platforms to reach the lost? In order to answer this question, we realized it was time for

> If adults aren't being brought into the Church, it stands to reason that our regular methods of evangelism simply aren't working as they once did

more research. We needed honest answers about why people in our digital age are or are not sharing their faith, and to understand how we can help them share their faith more fruitfully in our new digital landscape.

In David Kinnaman and his Barna colleagues, we again found the right partner for finding up-to-date, real-world, research-based answers to our questions. Many of the findings from this first year of research confirm hypotheses we had formed based on trends we had nervously observed—but the findings also give us a lot to get excited about. Here are a few examples:

- Many of today's younger Christians feel a strong personal responsibility to share their faith.
- Christians are having more and more faith conversations through social media and other digital avenues.
- An increasing number of Christians say they are most comfortable sharing their faith within the warmth of friendship using genuine conversation and dialogue.
- Most encouraging, people who share their faith these days typically feel joy and are energized to share even more. Outreach begets outreach, even in our changing times.

Taken in the aggregate, the potential these findings reveal is good news for the cause of the gospel in our day.

Last year I traveled to one of Lutheran Hour Ministries' overseas ministry centers and witnessed the baptism of 36 people, both adults and children. These baptisms took place under a mango tree in a Kenyan village, the spot where the local church holds its worship services. As the congregation danced and sang in celebration, I realized that these 36 new Christians weren't introduced to Christ by a grandiose structure or a lone hard-working pastor. No, it was lay members of their community, reaching out to their neighbors in love, who shared the gospel with them.

The research you're about to read demonstrates that in North America, we've got a bit of an uphill battle to get to that point—but also that it is possible. If we can learn how to plant the gospel seed effectively in our new digital world, we may not be so far from celebrating our own influx of new Christian brothers and sisters on a Sunday morning.

At Lutheran Hour Ministries, we are committed to doing just that. I invite you to read on and join us on this mission.

Many of today's younger Christians feel a strong personal responsibility to share their fath

INTRODUCTION

BY ROXANNE STONE

Editor in Chief of Barna Group

When was the last time you had a conversation about God?

Because you are reading this book, I'm going to guess it was fairly recently. Maybe even today. If so, you are among a very small percentage of Americans. Fewer than one in 10 talks about God, faith, religion or spirituality even once a week (8%)—and only an additional 15 percent do so once a month. In fact, the average adult says they only have about one spiritual conversation a year.

Okay, you say, that's low . . . but that's among *all* Americans. What about among Christians? Surely the people of God are talking about faith regularly?

The answer, unfortunately and surprisingly, is *not really*. Three-quarters of self-identified U.S. Christians are what we call *reluctant conversationalists* (more on this group throughout the book): They are having fewer than 10 spiritual conversations a year. In other words, for most Christians in the U.S., topics of faith come up *less than once a month*.

As spiritual leaders and practitioners, whose job it is to think and talk about matters of faith, it's easy to imagine everyone is regularly doing the same. After all, aren't these *the* big questions of life? Don't these topics matter more than anything else?

The truth is, most Christians are busy with other things: the day-to-day of normal life—jobs, kids, budgets, sports, weather and what's premiering on Netflix this week. None of this is bad, but the unfortunate reality is that most adults don't seem to connect their everyday experiences with their faith. Or, at least, they aren't talking about it if they do.

This stands in direct contrast to the vision Paul offers Christians in his epistle to the Romans:

> Most adults don't seem to connect their everyday experiences with their faith—or if they do, they aren't talking about it

So here's what I want you to do, God helping you: Take your everyday, ordinary life—your sleeping, eating, going-to-work, and walking-around life—and place it before God as an offering. Embracing what God does for you is the best thing you can do for him. Don't become so well-adjusted to your culture that you fit into it without even thinking. Instead, fix your attention on God. You'll be changed from the inside out. Readily recognize what he wants from you, and quickly respond to it. Unlike the culture around you, always dragging you down to its level of immaturity, God brings the best out of you, developed well-formed maturity in you."

(Romans 12:1–2, MSG)

So what's happening here? Why are Christians so reluctant to talk about their faith?

Based on Barna's extensive research on faith and religion over the past three-plus decades, we can identify some overarching cultural trends that are undoubtedly contributing to a society that is less interested in religion and that has marginalized the place of spirituality in everyday life.

SECULARISM

It may come as no surprise that the influence of Christianity in the United States is waning. Rates of church attendance, religious affiliation, belief in God, prayer and Bible reading have been dropping for decades. By consequence, the role of religion in public life has been slowly diminishing, and Christianity no longer functions with the cultural authority it held in times past. These are unique days for the Church in North America as it learns what it means to flourish in a new post-Christian era.

Barna has developed a metric to measure the changing religious landscape of the broader culture. We call this the "post-Christian metric." To qualify as post-Christian, individuals must meet 9 or more of 16 criteria, which identify a lack of Christian identity, belief and practice. These factors include whether individuals identify as atheist, have never made a commitment to

These are unique days for the Church in North America as it learns how to flourish in a post-Christian era

Jesus, have not attended church in the last year and have not read the Bible in the last week.

These kinds of questions—compared to checking the "Christian" box in a census or survey—get beyond how people loosely identify themselves (affiliation) to the core of what they actually believe and how they behave as a result of their beliefs (practice). Asking these questions gives us a much fuller picture of belief and unbelief in America.

Over recent years we've seen the percentage of Americans who qualify as post-Christian steadily rise: from 37 percent of U.S. adults in 2013 to 44 percent in 2018.

This rise in secularism, coupled with growing skepticism toward the Bible and Christianity creates a cultural climate in which talk of spiritual or religious matters becomes less pertinent and less comfortable. In such a society, public and private life are inevitably less affected by and less tinted with thoughts of God and the implications of faith.

> The percentage of Americans who qualify as post-Christian has risen from 37% in 2013 to 44% in 2018

RELATIVISM

"You do you." It's a common enough phrase these days, and it neatly sums up one of the more pervasive ideas of this second decade in the 21st century: *Who am I to judge what you do with your life?* It's a sentiment rooted in both individuality and relativism. America has long celebrated the sovereignty of the individual when it comes to personal decisions and lifestyle. However, as belief in objective truth claims (outside of scientific evidence) have waned, the individual's domain has expanded to include adjudication of moral truth as well. A few examples from recent Barna studies:

- Only 35% of Americans agree that moral truth is absolute (44% say it's relative; 21% admit to never having thought about it)
- 91% say the best way to find yourself is by looking within yourself
- 79% say people can believe whatever they want, as long as those beliefs don't affect society
- 57% say whatever is right for your life or works best for you is the only truth you can know
- 60% believe it is "extreme" to attempt to convert others to your faith

It is harder and harder to challenge someone's beliefs on the basis of claims about objective truth. This makes spiritual conversations more tepid—after all, everyone can just believe whatever they want and it makes no difference, right? People are instead seeking what works for their life, with less concern for whether these beliefs and practices are rooted in a universal truth—and whether anyone else agrees with them.

PLURALISM & THE FEAR OF OFFENSE

Unfortunately, the message of Christianity has not always been wielded with grace. Many people know Christianity more for what it's against than what it is for. To be against something (or *someone*) is frowned upon in America today, whether that's women's reproductive rights, same-sex marriage or the efficacy of another religion.

Tolerance is the word of the day—and while tolerance is certainly a beneficial virtue in a pluralistic society where we must find a way to live alongside one another, walking the fine line between tolerance and one's convictions is a difficult challenge for many Christians.

Fear of giving offense is one of the primary barriers for many Christians when it comes to talking about their faith

Indeed, you will see in the pages of this book that a fear of giving offense or being rejected is one of the primary barriers for many Christians when it comes to talking about their faith. The number-one reason they don't have more spiritual conversations is because "religious conversations always seem to create tension or arguments."

In surveys for Barna president David Kinnaman's book *Good Faith*, practicing Christians admit that when it comes to their faith in society today, they feel misunderstood (65%), persecuted (60%), marginalized (48%), silenced (46%) and afraid to speak up (47%).

When nearly half of practicing Christians feel afraid to speak up about their faith, it is no wonder fewer and fewer are doing so.

THE DIGITAL AGE

There is another major factor affecting our world today and the conversations we're having with each other: technology. The impact of the internet, and of social media, on our daily lives cannot be overstated.

Barna and our research partner, Lutheran Hour Ministries, wanted to understand how spiritual conversations have changed as society has changed. We wanted to know: *How are people talking about God in this new digital age?*

In 1993 Barna conducted a study on evangelism with Lutheran Hour Ministries. We decided to replicate parts of that study to measure some of the shifts that have occurred over the past 25 years. In addition, we wanted to broaden the scope of the research beyond just evangelism to any kind of conversation about God, faith, religion or spirituality.

We designed a multi-part study that included qualitative research as well as a nationally representative quantitative survey. (For a complete research methodology, see Appendix B.) Our goal for the research, and the report you're reading now, was to get a sense of how Americans talk with each other about matters of faith, including:

- **Frequency:** How often do people have spiritual conversations?
- **Personal responsibility:** Do Christians believe they are called to talk about their faith?
- **Technology:** How has social media impacted the ways Christians share their beliefs?
- **Experiences:** What happens when people talk about God? How do they feel when they share their beliefs? How do they feel when someone else shares their beliefs with them?
- **Methods:** In what ways do people talk about their faith?
- **Who is sharing:** What makes someone more likely to talk about their beliefs with others?

In these pages, we share our findings and offer insights from our researchers, as well as from outside contributors whose expertise shine different angles of light on the challenges of having spiritual conversations in the digital age. We believe Christ's followers have something essential and meaningful to share with their families, neighbors, friends and those they come into contact with. We want to see churches come alongside believers and empower them with confidence to talk about their faith. We want to see Christians begin to make the connections between their everyday, ordinary life—their sleeping, eating, going-to-work and walking-around life—and the faith that sustains them. And we want to them to tell others the good news of Jesus.

Let the conversation begin.

> We want to see churches come alongside believers and empower them with confidence to talk about their faith

SPIRITUAL CONVERSATIONS AT A GLANCE

One-third of all U.S. adults say they have made a "big change" in their life because of a conversation about faith (35%).

1 in 3 Christians says someone has come to believe in Jesus after they shared about their faith in him.

In 1993, nine out of 10 Christians agreed that "every Christian has a responsibility to share their faith" (89%). Today, just two-thirds say so (64%) . . . a 25-point drop.

Millennials (65%) and Gen X (67%) are more likely than Boomers (60%) to agree sharing one's faith is every Christian's responsibility.

1 in 4 Christians has had 10 or more conversations about faith in the past year (27%).

3 out of 4 Christians have had fewer than 10 such conversations during the past year (74%).

More than half agree that "technology and digital interactions have made sharing my faith easier" (53%)—yet about the same percentage says that "people are more likely to avoid real spiritual conversations than they were in the past because they are so busy with technology" (55%).

Nearly half of Christians admit they would avoid a spiritual conversation if it meant their non-Christian friend would reject them (45%).

A majority of practicing Christians (61%), non-practicing Christians (55%) and non-Christians (55%) choose "a friend" as the person they most want to talk with about faith.

CHANGES IN SPIRITUAL CONVERSATIONS OVER 25 YEARS

TODAY, CHRISTIANS ARE LESS LIKELY TO...

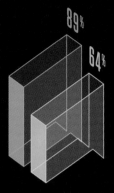

89% 64%

Believe every Christian has a responsibility to share their faith

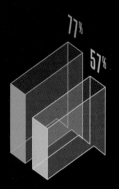

77% 57%

Claim their church does a good job of training people to share their faith

77% 65%

Share by the way they live, rather than speaking about it

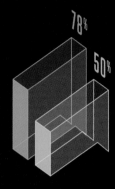

78% 50%

Speak about the changes / benefits of accepting Jesus

THEY ARE MORE LIKELY THAN 25 YEARS AGO TO...

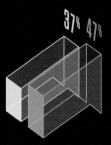

37% 47%

Believe sharing their faith is only effective if they have a relationship with the person

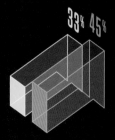

33% 45%

Avoid discussions about faith if their non-Christian friend would reject them

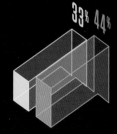

33% 44%

Use the same basic approach and content each time they share their faith

11% 19%

Actively seek / create opportunities to share their faith

● ● ● 1993

● ● ● Today

57% **45%**

Tell the story of how they first came to believe in Jesus

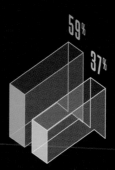

59% **37%**

Quote passages from the Bible when sharing their faith

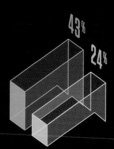

43% **24%**

Challenge someone to defend their beliefs

CHRISTIANS ARE ABOUT AS LIKELY TODAY AS IN 1993 TO...

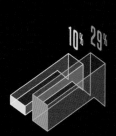

10% **29%**

Say converting people to Christianity is the job of the local church

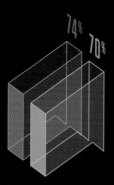

74% **70%**

Ask questions about their beliefs / experiences when sharing their faith

53% **45%**

Pray for the person before they get together

45% **48%**

Say that most non-Christians have no interest in hearing about Jesus

1993: *n*=446 Christians who have had a conversation about their faith, August 14–20, 1993.

Today: *n*=796 Christians who have had a conversation about their faith, June 22–July 13, 2017.

SHARING FAITH THEN & NOW

1

The landscape of Christian faith in America has changed dramatically in the past 25 years. Most people have at least heard mention of the rising percentage of "nones"—those who do not identify with any religious faith—especially in the Millennial generation and younger. Religious identity is undergoing a massive, culture-wide shift.

Even more than shifting religious identity, engagement in faith *practices* has changed. For example, in 1993, more than two-thirds of U.S. self-identified Christians reported attending a church worship service within the past week (68%). Today, just 40 percent of Christians say they went to church last Sunday. So even among adults who still check the "Christian" box, church attendance is becoming more rare.

THEN & NOW: CHURCH ATTENDANCE AMONG CHRISTIANS

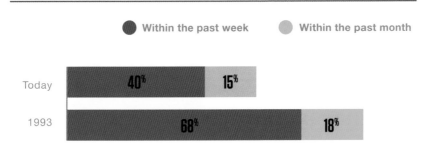

● Within the past week   ● Within the past month

Today   40%   15%

1993   68%   18%

Ideas and practices surrounding evangelism—Christians sharing the gospel of Christ with non-Christians—have likewise changed. A growing number of Christians don't see sharing the good news as a personal responsibility.

As the chart shows, just 10 percent of Christians in 1993 who had shared about their faith agreed with the statement "converting people to Christianity is the job of the local church"—as opposed to the job of an individual (i.e., themselves). Twenty-five years later, three in 10 Christians who have had a conversation about faith say evangelism is the local church's responsibility (29%), a nearly threefold increase. This jump could be the result of many factors, including poor ecclesiology (believing "the local church" is somehow separate from the people who are a part of it), personal and cultural barriers to sharing faith (explored at length in the next chapter) and insufficient training. In fact, with regard to training, the percentage of Christians who say their church does a good job in this area has declined significantly since 1993: Three-quarters said so then (77%), compared to fewer than six in 10 now (57%).

THEN & NOW: WHAT CHRISTIANS BELIEVE ABOUT EVANGELISM

% AMONG CHRISTIANS WHO HAVE HAD A CONVERSATION ABOUT THEIR FAITH

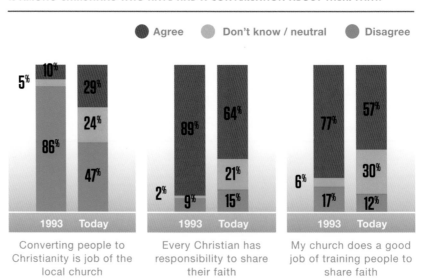

● Agree   ● Don't know / neutral   ● Disagree

Converting people to Christianity is job of the local church

Every Christian has responsibility to share their faith

My church does a good job of training people to share faith

1993: n=446 Christians who have had a conversation about their faith, August 14–20, 1993;
Today: n=796 Christians who have had a conversation about their faith, June 22–July 13, 2017.

Yet the most dramatic divergence over time is on the statement, "Every Christian has a responsibility to share their faith." In 1993, nine out of 10 Christians who had shared their faith agreed (89%). Today, just two-thirds say so (64%)—a 25-point drop.

Millennial (65%) and Gen X (67%) Christians are most likely to agree that sharing one's faith is every Christ-follower's responsibility, compared to Boomers (60%) and Elders (55%). Likewise, younger Christians are more likely to agree they have a personal responsibility to share their faith. Some may find these data points hard to believe at first glance, since young adults dropping out of church and even faith is a well-documented trend. But Barna's findings on generational faith-sharing have been consistent over the past several years: In 2013, in fact, analysts published an online article that asserts, "For Millennials, the practice of evangelism is notably on the rise."[1]

It is both true that many Christian young adults drop out of church involvement *and* true that those who remain tend to be especially passionate about and tenacious in their faith. The percentage of Millennial Christians is lower than among other generations—yet they are passionate and committed.

> Many Christian young adults drop out of church involvement— but those who remain tend to be especially passionate about their faith

CONVERSATION STARTERS

Barna's 1993 research on evangelism was, in many respects, quite specific. Researchers asked people whether, in the past year, they had explained "your religious beliefs to someone who you felt had different beliefs, in the hope that they might accept Jesus as their savior." If they answered yes, the survey continued—so only those who had directly engaged in Christian evangelism were interviewed.

At the outset of the new research on which this report is based, Barna and Lutheran Hour Ministries wanted to widen the lens in order to get a broader, fuller picture of spiritual conversations overall. Researchers asked U.S. adults how often they have had "a conversation about your faith (or lack of faith) with anyone in the past year." These conversations may not necessarily have involved an intention to persuade someone to convert. Nearly half of all Americans say they have had from zero to two such conversations in the past year (45%); one-third says between three and nine (33%); and 23 percent say they have been part of 10 or more faith conversations in the past 12 months.

NUMBER OF CONVERSATIONS ABOUT FAITH IN THE PAST YEAR

% AMONG U.S. SELF-IDENTIFIED CHRISTIANS

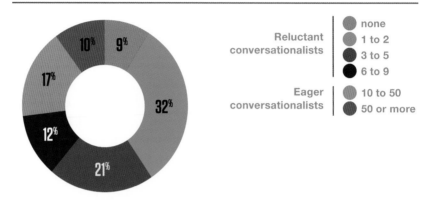

Reluctant conversationalists
- none
- 1 to 2
- 3 to 5
- 6 to 9

Eager conversationalists
- 10 to 50
- 50 or more

n=796 U.S. self-identified Christians, June 22–July 13, 2017.

27% of U.S. Christians share their faith 10 or more times in a year

Let's zero in on self-identified Christians. At the polar extremes, one in 11 reports zero spiritual conversations in the past year, while one in 10 says they have had 50 or more (that's nearly one per week).

In order to understand what, if anything, distinguishes Christians who talk often about faith from those who don't, researchers created two categories: eager conversationalists (who have had 10 or more spiritual conversations in the past year) and reluctant conversationalists (nine or fewer spiritual conversations). One-quarter of Christians is eager (27%) while the other three out of four are reluctant (74%).

It's true that Christians are not the only people in America talking about faith—but interest overall appears to be low. One in five adherents to a religion other than Christianity says they have had 10 or more spiritual conversations in the past year (21%), and one in 10 atheists, agnostics or "nones"—the religiously unaffiliated (10%)—says the same. All together, about one in eight non-Christians appears eager to talk about their faith or lack thereof (12%).

WHAT & WHEN THEY SHARE

From 1993 to today, the content and approaches of faith conversations have also changed. Given the popularity of evangelism "programs" or "strategies" in decades past, analysts were somewhat surprised that Christians today who have talked about their faith are more likely than those in 1993 to say they use the same basic approach and content each time they engage in a conversation about faith (44% vs. 33%).

The most common approaches, a majority says, are asking questions about the other person's beliefs and experiences (70%) and sharing their faith in the way they live rather than by speaking about it (65%). These were common among Christians in 1993 as well, as the chart shows, but a majority of Christians 25 years ago also reported emphasizing the beneficial aspects of accepting Jesus (78%)—a strategy that today is less common (50%). Also less popular now compared to then is quoting passages from the Bible (59% in 1993 vs. 37% today) and challenging the other person to defend their beliefs (43% vs. 24%).

THEN & NOW: CONTENT AND APPROACHES FOR SHARING FAITH

% AMONG CHRISTIANS WHO HAVE HAD A CONVERSATION ABOUT THEIR FAITH

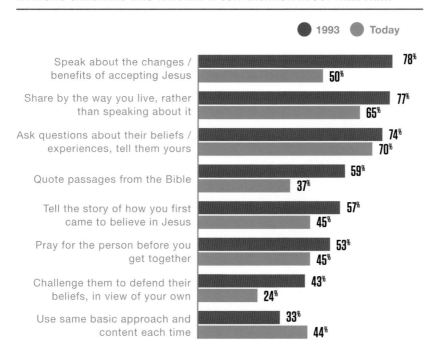

● 1993   ● Today

Speak about the changes / benefits of accepting Jesus — 78% / 50%
Share by the way you live, rather than speaking about it — 77% / 65%
Ask questions about their beliefs / experiences, tell them yours — 74% / 70%
Quote passages from the Bible — 59% / 37%
Tell the story of how you first came to believe in Jesus — 57% / 45%
Pray for the person before you get together — 53% / 45%
Challenge them to defend their beliefs, in view of your own — 43% / 24%
Use same basic approach and content each time — 33% / 44%

1993: *n*=446 Christians who have had a conversation about their faith, August 14–20, 1993;
Today: *n*=796 Christians who have had a conversation about their faith, June 22–July 13, 2017.

When it comes to sharing his faith through the way he lives his life, one Christian expressed the idea this way in answer to an open-ended question: "I try to live my faith in my everyday dealings with people and in my conversations—not by standing on a street corner and preaching, or going door to door and bothering people."

A woman testified to the importance of prayer to her spiritual conversations: "My faith continues to grow as I am tested and becoming more like Jesus. He gives me a love for people, and I pray for opportunity to share this good news with people I meet along the way."

She is not alone in actively looking for opportunities to share her faith. Most conversations today (61%), as in 1993 (75%), happen unexpectedly. Yet compared to 25 years ago, Christians today are more likely to say they are proactive about looking for or trying to create faith-sharing opportunities with non-Christians (19% vs. 11% in 1993).

Eager conversationalists are, not surprisingly, more likely than reluctant conversationalists to actively seek sharing opportunities. One-quarter says they are often on the lookout for chances to talk about their faith (27%), compared to just 15 percent of those who share infrequently.

More Christians today say they are proactive about looking for faith-sharing opportunities

THEN & NOW: OPPORTUNITIES TO SHARE FAITH

% AMONG CHRISTIANS WHO HAVE HAD A CONVERSATION ABOUT THEIR FAITH

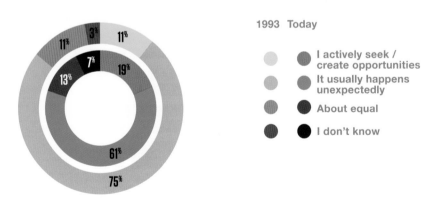

1993 Today

- I actively seek / create opportunities
- It usually happens unexpectedly
- About equal
- I don't know

1993: *n*=446 Christians who have had a conversation about their faith, August 14–20, 1993;

Today: *n*=796 Christians who have had a conversation about their faith, June 22–July 13, 2017.

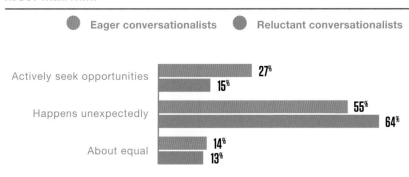

**OPPORTUNITIES TO SHARE FAITH,
BY NUMBER OF CONVERSATIONS**

*% AMONG SELF-IDENTIFIED CHRISTIANS WHO HAVE HAD A CONVERSATION
ABOUT THEIR FAITH*

● Eager conversationalists   ● Reluctant conversationalists

Actively seek opportunities — 27% / 15%
Happens unexpectedly — 55% / 64%
About equal — 14% / 13%

n=796 U.S. self-identified Christians, June 22–July 13, 2017.

BARRIERS TO FAITH-SHARING

Christians today, more than 25 years ago, perceive social barriers to sharing their faith. They are more likely to agree that faith-sharing is only effective when they already have a relationship with the other person (47% vs. 37% in 1993), and to admit they would avoid a spiritual conversation if they knew their non-Christian friend would reject them (44% vs. 33%). They are also more likely than Christians in 1993 to say they are unsure whether "most non-Christians have no interest in hearing about Jesus" (28% vs. 5%).

Christians today are not wrong in perceiving increased social risks.

In his book *Good Faith,* Barna president David Kinnaman dives deep into the shifting cultural currents surrounding people of faith and perceptions of how they practice their religious convictions. Research for that book found that a startling six in 10 Americans believe that any "attempt to convert others" to one's own faith is "extreme." More than eight out of 10 "nones" say so! To be clear: A majority of U.S. adults, and the vast majority of non-religious adults (83%), believe that evangelism is religiously extreme.[2]

This is the social backdrop against which U.S. adults judge when it is acceptable to have a conversation about a particular topic. In order to understand whether it's only religious topics on which Americans are reluctant to share their opinions, Barna also asked about a variety of other topics people

> 6 in 10 Americans believe that any attempt to convert others to one's own faith is "extreme"

THEN & NOW: CHRISTIANS' SOCIAL PERCEPTIONS OF FAITH-SHARING

% AMONG CHRISTIANS WHO HAVE HAD A CONVERSATION ABOUT THEIR FAITH

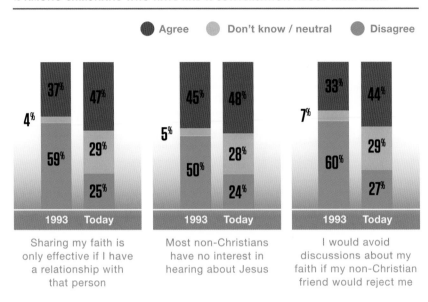

● Agree　　● Don't know / neutral　　● Disagree

	1993	Today
Sharing my faith is only effective if I have a relationship with that person	37% / 59% / 4%	47% / 29% / 25%

	1993	Today
Most non-Christians have no interest in hearing about Jesus	45% / 50% / 5%	48% / 28% / 24%

	1993	Today
I would avoid discussions about my faith if my non-Christian friend would reject me	33% / 60% / 7%	44% / 29% / 27%

1993: *n*=446 Christians who have had a conversation about their faith, August 14–20, 1993;
Today: *n*=796 Christians who have had a conversation about their faith, June 22–July 13, 2017.

> **Non-Christians tend to have more of a "buyer beware" stance when it comes to religion compared to other topics**

engage in conversations about—ranging from the rather banal (parenting, health) to the controversial (politics, LBGTQ issues). Researchers asked if there are conditions that might make a conversation about these topics and issues unacceptable. Non-Christians tend to have more of a "buyer beware" stance when it comes to religion compared to the other topics. They are more likely to say talking about one's religious beliefs is "always unacceptable" (7%) than to say so about health (1%) or LGBTQ issues (4%). On the flip side, practicing Christians are twice as likely as non-Christians to say there is never a time when sharing religious beliefs should be off the table—that is, spiritual conversations are always acceptable (26% vs. 12% non-Christians). On the other topics, however, practicing Christians tend to be more reticent than non-Christians: 11 percent say it is "always unacceptable" to share views on LGBTQ issues and 5 percent say so about health.

Q&A WITH ANTHONY COOK

Rev. Dr. Anthony Cook is Executive Director of United States Ministries for Lutheran Hour Ministries. He has served as a parish pastor and advised numerous organizations on curriculum design and development, distance learning, internet technologies and sharing the gospel through various forms of multimedia. Tony served as Associate Professor of Practical Theology at Concordia Seminary, specializing in education, pastoral theology plus leadership and postmodern studies, including courses on preaching to postmoderns, post-liberal theology and emerging Christianity. He also served as Concordia Seminary's Director of Curriculum Design and Development.

Many Christians are feeling more hesitant to share their faith, compared to Christians 25 years ago. In your view, what tools and skills could help believers feel more confident and prepared?

First, we can remind ourselves what exactly it is we are called by God to do. We are not called to convince, cajole or convert. We are simply called, as 1 Peter 3:15–16 states, to revere Christ as Lord and be prepared to gently and respectfully give the reason for the hope that lies within us. That's it. The more we free ourselves from false responsibility of "converting others," the less fearful and hesitant we can be.

Second, we can learn how to gain a hearing for the gospel before we start sharing it. In a world where personal perspectives rule, we gain a hearing by engaging in spiritual conversations that are open, honest and conducted within the warm light of friendship. This approach helps us earn the right to share our faith, opening the door for God to do his work.

Finally, we can practice connecting stories from our everyday life with the story of salvation in Jesus. Learning to see and narrate our everyday life through the redemptive lens of God's grace helps us to share the gospel more naturally and relevantly. Christianity is more than a belief system. It is a way of life.

? Given your expertise in education and background in pastoral ministry, what are your thoughts about how church leaders can effectively equip Christians for sharing faith?

Evangelism training has traditionally focused on providing the learner with an understanding of the salvation narrative, techniques for sharing that narrative and basic apologetics. This, however, is not enough. Equipping Christians to have spiritual conversations is a multifaceted process involving all three educational domains: cognitive, affective and behavioral. While the knowledge and skills we've traditionally focused on are certainly important, they are of little worth if the learner is not motived to use them. Learner motivation is one of the most overlooked aspects of Christian education.

So where does motivation come from? I was once told that "people do what people want to do"—in other words, people do what they value. Value development is at the heart of motivating Christians to have spiritual conversations and is a vital component in any equipping process. But it is neither quick nor easy. Developing values related to spiritual conversations means helping Christians to develop an awareness of spiritual conversations, to acknowledge their importance, to commit to engaging in them, to organize their priorities in order to make time for such conversations and to talk about spiritual matters in a natural and consistent manner.

A Christian is not equipped to share the gospel of Jesus Christ unless the value of engaging in spiritual conversations in their daily lives has been instilled within them.

? There is a clear connection between strong spiritual practices and an eagerness to engage in faith conversations. Why do you believe these two are linked? How do you see them feeding into each other?

The rhythm of engaging in both spiritual practices and spiritual conversations creates a powerful virtuous cycle. We strengthen faith by sharing it with others. Over the years, I have come to believe that evangelism is not something that should be reserved for the mature in faith. Instead, it is at the core of the maturation process itself. When Christians are intentionally involved in both spiritual practices and spiritual conversations, faith deepens and eagerness to share that faith grows.

Why does the connection work? I believe the answer is both theological and sociological. Theologically, we know that the Holy Spirit is at work in both spiritual practices and spiritual conversations. As the Holy Spirit works through God's word, he strengthens and sanctifies us in the faith. In fact, living our daily lives immersed in the word of God is at the heart of the Christian life.

Sociologically, we have learned that when we are exposed to the salvation narrative we begin to take that narrative on as our own. Over time, it shapes our identity, values and ultimately behaviors, giving us a new way to see ourselves and the world around us. This change in identity and perspective is further strengthened and solidified as we give voice to that narrative. In the end, the more we share our faith, the more we understand who we are and the more confident and eager we become as Christians.

SHARING VIEWS ON THREE TOPICS

% AMONG U.S. ADULTS

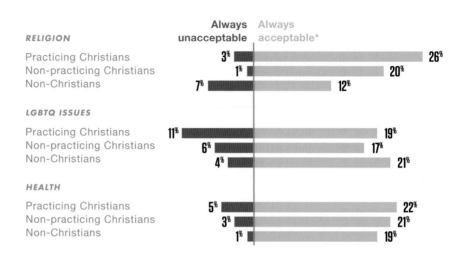

Always unacceptable | Always acceptable*

RELIGION

Practicing Christians — 3% | 26%
Non-practicing Christians — 1% | 20%
Non-Christians — 7% | 12%

LGBTQ ISSUES

Practicing Christians — 11% | 19%
Non-practicing Christians — 6% | 17%
Non-Christians — 4% | 21%

HEALTH

Practicing Christians — 5% | 22%
Non-practicing Christians — 3% | 21%
Non-Christians — 1% | 19%

*"Never unacceptable" was the option in the survey; it has been changed here for clarity.
n=1,070 U.S. adults, June 22–July 13, 2017.

When it comes to specific conditions that make talking about delicate subjects unacceptable, non-Christians are again more cautious about religion than about the other topics. Six out of 10 say a person must not share if their religious beliefs are "disrespectful or judgmental" (61%), compared to just over half who say so about health topics (53%). Beliefs perceived as disrespectful or judgmental are the top reason sharing would be uncalled for on all three potentially hot topics: About half of all adults agree (46% health, 45% LGBTQ issues, 48% religion). This is the case for all faith categories, including Christians, but they are less likely than non-Christians to say so. (It is unclear who would have final say on whether a belief is disrespectful or judgmental, but most people agree that disrespect or judgment is a deal-breaker.)

Practicing Christians seem to be more concerned than other groups about what's going on inside the person who is sharing; 41 percent say talking about faith in anger makes sharing unacceptable. On the other hand, one practicing Christian in qualitative research explained that, in her view, it is

41% of practicing Christians say talking about faith in anger makes sharing unacceptable

WHEN SHARING VIEWS ON RELIGION IS UNACCEPTABLE

% AMONG U.S. ADULTS

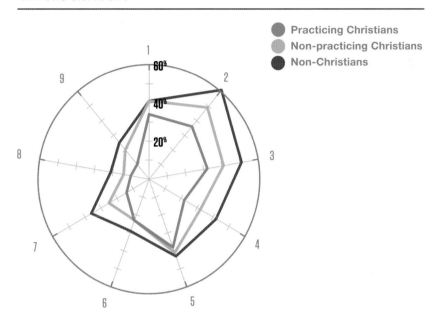

● Practicing Christians
● Non-practicing Christians
● Non-Christians

1. If it is untrue
2. If it is disrespectful or judgmental
3. If someone has asked you not to

4. If the timing is inconsiderate
5. If shared in anger
6. If it causes someone else to react in a bad way

7. If beliefs are shared as if they applied to everyone
8. If the other person can't respond
9. If discussed during work hours

n=1,070 U.S. adults, June 22–July 13, 2017.

not acceptable to share about faith "when [the other person is] not ready to hear it; when talking about faith will only antagonize and harden someone's thoughts against God."

This group has to live in a tension not often felt by others: between Jesus' commands to tell others the good news and growing cultural taboos against proselytizing. Evangelism has been a core part of Christianity from its origins and, many practicing Christians believe, is essential for the salvation of their listeners. But if your listeners just don't want to hear? That is a difficult—but not impossible!—barrier to surmount.

WHY AMERICANS DON'T TALK ABOUT GOD

% ALL ADULTS

CONVERSATIONS ABOUT FAITH (OR LACK OF FAITH) ARE MORE *INFREQUENT*...

...THAN *FREQUENT*

- No conversations in past year
- 1–2 conversations in past year
- 3–5 conversations in past year

- 6–9 conversations in past year
- 10–50 conversations in past year
- 50+ conversations in past year

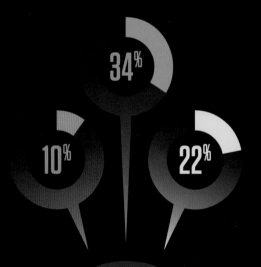

34%

10%

22%

15% *

11%

8% *

* Less than one-quarter of Americans discusses faith even once a month

IT'S UNACCEPTABLE TO SHARE YOUR VIEWS ON RELIGION...

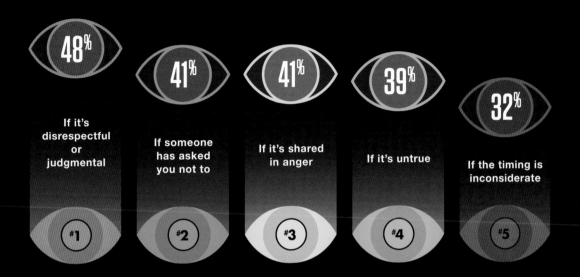

48% If it's disrespectful or judgmental #1

41% If someone has asked you not to #2

41% If it's shared in anger #3

39% If it's untrue #4

32% If the timing is inconsiderate #5

6 / 10 CHRISTIAN MILLENNIALS SAY PEOPLE ARE MORE LIKELY NOW THAN IN THE PAST TO SEE THEM AS OFFENSIVE IF THEY SHARE THEIR FAITH

(TWICE AS LIKELY AS CHRISTIAN BOOMERS)

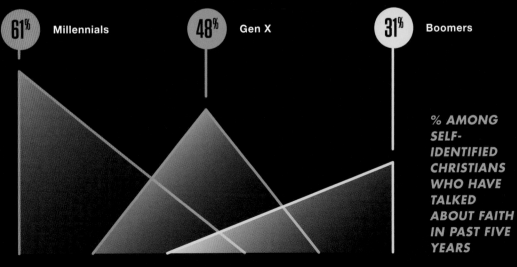

61% Millennials

48% Gen X

31% Boomers

% AMONG SELF-IDENTIFIED CHRISTIANS WHO HAVE TALKED ABOUT FAITH IN PAST FIVE YEARS

n=1,070 U.S. adults. June 22–July 13, 2017.

Now that we have a lay of the spiritual-conversation landscape, let's look more deeply at the media people use to talk about faith, especially online and through mobile devices—because, of the many things that have changed since 1993, how we communicate and connect with each other may be the most significant.

DIGITAL FAITH INTERACTIONS

2

One massive and obvious change since 1993 is widespread use of the internet, social media and mobile devices. Many people got their first email address and / or cell phone in the 1990s (remember AOL and flip phones?) and shared a dial-up desktop computer with their entire family. Today, most people carry around a phone-size computer in their pocket and use it to connect with everyone from their spouse and children to their best friend from second grade who they haven't seen in 40 years.

The way we communicate has evolved—and, inevitably, so has the way we communicate about faith.

A considerable majority of all U.S. adults say they use Facebook (84%). Practicing Christians appear to be especially fond of the platform, with nine out of 10 reporting they use it (90%)—six percentage points more than non-practicing Christians (84%) and 11 more than non-Christians (79%).

Christian in-depth survey participants reported using social media for a variety of reasons, most of which had to do with staying connected to friends and family, often through sharing photos. Others said they use social media to get news, to counsel and encourage others, to keep up with organizations they like and to share their faith.

Based on the quantitative study, many U.S. adults who have engaged in spiritual conversations in the past five years report using social media and various other digital means, but face-to-face conversations still outpace them all. Nine out of 10 Americans who have shared their views on faith or religion have done so in person (92%). Half as many say they have shared on Facebook

9 out of 10 practicing Christians use Facebook

USE OF SOCIAL MEDIA PLATFORMS

% AMONG U.S. ADULTS

● All adults   ● Non-practicing Christians
● Practicing Christians   ● Non-Christians

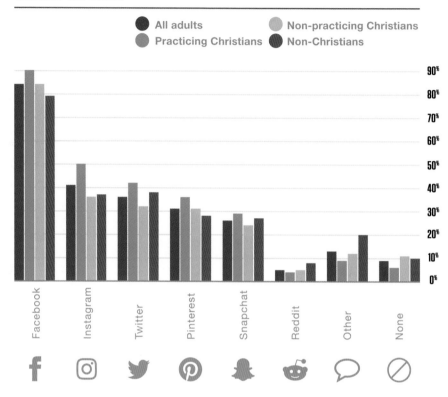

n=1,070 U.S. adults, June 22–July 13, 2017.

(43%), and such sharing is more common among self-identified Christians (46%) than among non-Christians (32%). Practicing Christians are even more likely to post faith-related content on Facebook (53%). Relatedly, eager conversationalists are more apt than those who are reluctant to use any and all of the options.

As one might expect, there are some significant differences between generations. For example, half of Elders say they have shared faith views in an email (52%)—only about one in five younger adults have done so. But two out of five Millennials have engaged in a text conversation about faith (39%), compared to three in 10 Gen X (29%), one in five Boomers (20%) and one in six Elders (18%).

2 out of 5
Millennials
have had a text
conversation
about faith

HOW I HAVE SHARED FAITH VIEWS *AND* HOW OTHERS
HAVE SHARED FAITH VIEWS WITH ME

% AMONG U.S. ADULTS WHO HAVE HAD A CONVERSATION ABOUT THEIR FAITH

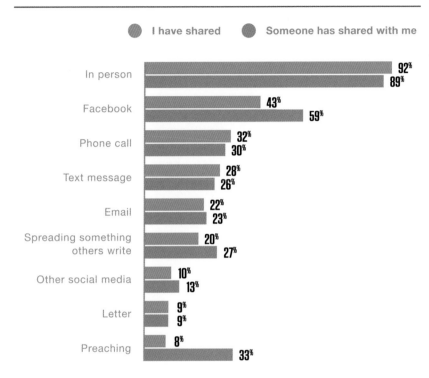

● I have shared   ● Someone has shared with me

	I have shared	Someone has shared with me
In person	92%	89%
Facebook	43%	59%
Phone call	32%	30%
Text message	28%	26%
Email	22%	23%
Spreading something others write	20%	27%
Other social media	10%	13%
Letter	9%	9%
Preaching	8%	33%

"I have shared" *n*=840 U.S. adults, "someone else has shared" *n*=675 U.S. adults, June 22–July 13, 2017.

There are many ways to express your faith through social media: from posting a Christian symbol as your profile picture, to including a Bible verse in your personal information, to sharing faith-based articles or sending encouragements and prayers in response to friends' posts. So what are some of the most common ways people do so? More than eight out of 10 adults say they share their faith on social media by writing their own posts, sharing others' posts or commenting on others' posts. Half report their profile contains information about religious beliefs and three in 10 say their profile image conveys their faith views. While differences between the faith groups are not hugely significant, it appears that practicing Christians are particularly apt to engage in these ways and non-Christians less so.

GOD ON THE INTERNET

DIGITAL INTERACTIONS ARE CHANGING HOW WE TALK TO EACH OTHER ABOUT OUR FAITH—FOR BETTER AND WORSE

28% of self-identified Christians share their faith via social media.

30% of self-identified Christians say they are just as likely to share their religious beliefs online as in person. 12% are more likely to share their faith digitally.

58% of non-Christians* say someone has shared their faith with them through Facebook, 14% through other social media.

31% of self-identified Christians** use digital communications when sharing their faith with a non-Christian (email, links, videos, Facebook, etc.).

47% of self-identified Christians** agree "technology and digital interactions have changed how others respond when I share my faith."

44% of self-identified Christians** say technology and digital interactions have changed how they share their faith.

*Who have had someone share their faith with them in past five years. **Who have talked about their faith in past five years.*

THE GIVE AND TAKE OF DIGITAL EVANGELISM

● Millennials ● Gen X ● Boomers

58%
64%
39%
Technology and digital interactions have made sharing my faith easier

58%
53%
30%
Technology and digital interactions make me more careful about how and when I share my faith

HOW CHRISTIANS SHARE THEIR FAITH ONLINE

88% **PERSONAL POSTS**

86% **SHARING OTHERS' POSTS**

 **69%**
69%
60%

It's harder to have a private, one-on-one conversation now than in the past because people are so busy with phones and technology

 64%
60%
45%

People are more likely to avoid real spiritual conversations than they were in the past because they are so busy with technology

 85% **COMMENT ON OTHERS' POSTS OR WALLS**

 58% **PROFILE INFORMATION**

 34% **PROFILE IMAGE**

n=1,070 U.S. adults, June 22–July 13, 2017.

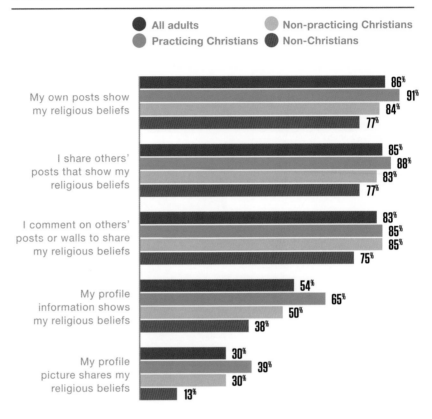

HOW I SHARE FAITH ON SOCIAL MEDIA

% AMONG U.S. ADULTS WHO SHARE RELIGIOUS VIEWS ON SOCIAL MEDIA

● All adults   ● Non-practicing Christians
● Practicing Christians   ● Non-Christians

My own posts show my religious beliefs
- 86%
- 91%
- 84%
- 77%

I share others' posts that show my religious beliefs
- 85%
- 88%
- 83%
- 77%

I comment on others' posts or walls to share my religious beliefs
- 83%
- 85%
- 85%
- 75%

My profile information shows my religious beliefs
- 54%
- 65%
- 50%
- 38%

My profile picture shares my religious beliefs
- 30%
- 39%
- 30%
- 13%

n=273 U.S. adults who have shared their faith on social media, June 22–July 13, 2017.

RISKS & REWARDS OF THE DIGITAL AGE

Millennials seem to most acutely feel the negative effects of technology, such as difficulty having authentic spiritual conversations

Does all this tech make sharing faith easier or harder? Or both, in different respects?

A majority of self-identified Christians believes technology impacts both how they share and how others engage with them. For example, more than half agree that "technology and digital interactions have made sharing my faith easier" (53%)—yet about the same percentage agrees that "people are more likely to avoid real spiritual conversations than they were in the past because they are so busy with technology" (55%).

Again, there are generational differences worth noting. As the chart shows, younger adults are more likely than Boomers to agree with any of the statements about digital faith interactions. (Elders are not included due to small sample size.) Millennials seem to most acutely feel the negative effects of technology, such as difficulty having authentic spiritual conversations.

CHRISTIAN GENERATIONS ON SHARING FAITH IN THE DIGITAL AGE

% AGREE AMONG SELF-IDENTIFIED CHRISTIANS WHO HAVE HAD A CONVERSATION ABOUT THEIR FAITH

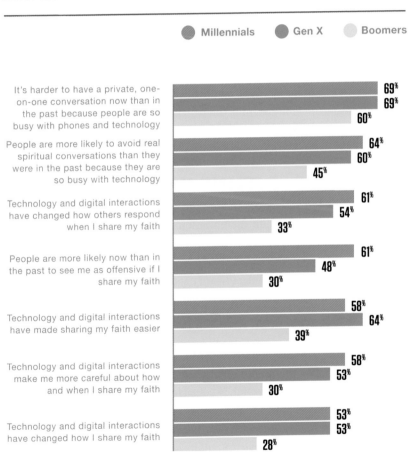

● Millennials ● Gen X ○ Boomers

It's harder to have a private, one-on-one conversation now than in the past because people are so busy with phones and technology
- 69%
- 69%
- 60%

People are more likely to avoid real spiritual conversations than they were in the past because they are so busy with technology
- 64%
- 60%
- 45%

Technology and digital interactions have changed how others respond when I share my faith
- 61%
- 54%
- 33%

People are more likely now than in the past to see me as offensive if I share my faith
- 61%
- 48%
- 30%

Technology and digital interactions have made sharing my faith easier
- 58%
- 64%
- 39%

Technology and digital interactions make me more careful about how and when I share my faith
- 58%
- 53%
- 30%

Technology and digital interactions have changed how I share my faith
- 53%
- 53%
- 28%

n=796 U.S. self-identified Christians, June 22–July 13, 2017.

In an interview for Barna's 2018 study on Gen Z, the generation after Millennials who are beginning to emerge into adulthood, scholar and author Donna Freitas remarked on the disconnect many young adults feel between their real lives and their digital lives:

> The goal for their social media presence seems to be about appearing happy at every turn—with all profiles that are attached to their real names. Appearing successful, appearing positive, never showing that you're vulnerable, never showing that you've failed at anything, never showing that you're sad. There's a kind of constant performance that's expected on social media.[3]

Part of equipping young adults to share faith effectively may need to include coaching them on how to have a healthy relationship with social media

This kind of performative pressure does not pair well with efforts to authentically connect with others on spiritual matters. For church and ministry leaders, part of equipping young adults to share faith effectively in the digital age may need to include coaching them on how to have a healthy relationship with social media, even before they start talking about faith.

ONLINE VS. OFFLINE INTERACTIONS

Researchers in the early years of the World Wide Web identified a phenomenon they termed the "online disinhibition effect": the tendency of people to do or say things online that they wouldn't normally do or say in real life.[4] One Christian wrote about the temptation to be more disrespectful online than he might be face to face, especially toward people he doesn't know: "If it's a good friend, I try to disagree respectfully and logically and with common sense. If it's someone I don't know I try to do the same, but I might use slightly harsher language, or even ridicule."

The online disinhibition phenomenon is well-documented by researchers yet often under-reported when left up to self-assessment; that is, most people would say their behavior is consistent between physical and digital space—but for many, it is not. Because of the disinhibition tendency, people who otherwise would speak with care and kindness may communicate more aggressively online. One in five U.S. adults admits they are more likely to "say something unkind" *digitally* (19%) than *in person* (41%)—but it's hard to know how strongly to rely on these self-reports.

All that being said, self-assessments can still yield useful insights. For example, U.S. adults were asked to choose whether they are more likely to engage in a certain type of interaction in person or digitally, or if they are equally likely to engage in either venue. Researchers expected that a majority or at least a plurality of people would say their behavior is consistent, that their behavior is "about the same" in both places. Thus we could think of "about the same" as the default answer—and indeed, that is what the research findings indicate.

But can we infer anything constructive about those who make a different choice? Analysts suggest that opting for "in person" or "digitally" may indicate a *preference* for that mode of communication. Those who choose one or the other may not be accurately *reporting* their behavior so much as signaling their preference for either digital or in-person interaction.

For example, as you can see in the chart broken out by gender, men are more likely than women to make a clear choice between in person or online for each of the interaction types. The point is not that men engage more than women in person or online, but that they are more likely than women to pick one or the other, and less likely to choose both.

LIKELIHOOD OF IN-PERSON VS. DIGITAL INTERACTIONS, WOMEN VS. MEN

% AMONG ALL U.S. ADULTS

● In person   ● About the same   ● Digitally

SHARE YOUR RELIGIOUS BELIEFS

	In person	About the same	Digitally
Women	44%	48%	9%
Men	52%	38%	11%

ASK A QUESTION ABOUT FAITH OR RELIGION

	In person	About the same	Digitally
Women	46%	47%	7%
Men	52%	38%	11%

n=1,070 U.S. adults, June 22–July 13, 2017.

Similarly, as the next chart shows, when it comes to asking questions about faith or sharing their beliefs, Millennials are more likely than older adults to make a choice other than the default—and, as one might expect from this tech-immersed generation, they are more likely to prefer digital interactions.

Where does all this data leave us?

First, it leaves us confident that, at least for now, face-to-face encounters remain the primary means by which people talk with others about faith. That could change as Gen Z and Millennials become a larger proportion of the overall adult population but, for the foreseeable future, the ability to have meaningful real-life conversations about spiritual matters is still a skill each Christian needs to develop.

Second, it hints at a near future when digital faith interactions become a standard component of most spiritual conversations. As more and more of our communications become digitally mediated, it is all but inevitable. So in addition to enriching in-person faith conversations, Christians also need wisdom for making meaningful virtual connections that bear spiritual fruit.

Christians
need wisdom
for making
meaningful virtual
connections that
bear spiritual fruit

LIKELIHOOD OF IN-PERSON VS. DIGITAL INTERACTIONS, MILLENNIALS VS. ALL OLDER ADULTS

% AMONG ALL U.S. ADULTS

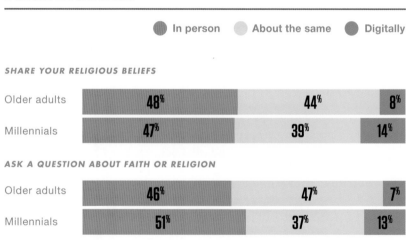

● In person   ● About the same   ● Digitally

SHARE YOUR RELIGIOUS BELIEFS

	In person	About the same	Digitally
Older adults	48%	44%	8%
Millennials	47%	39%	14%

ASK A QUESTION ABOUT FAITH OR RELIGION

	In person	About the same	Digitally
Older adults	46%	47%	7%
Millennials	51%	37%	13%

n=1,070 U.S. adults, June 22–July 13, 2017.

Third, it's important to recognize that, while many adults say they have about the same number of digital interactions as personal interactions, the nature of those interactions are likely quite different. An in-person conversation is immediate, reciprocal and informed by physical presence and body language. An online interaction is often much more terse, may or may not be two-sided and likely occurs while each person is engaged in other tasks or conversations. Additionally, it's much harder to translate tone, intent and context from an online interaction than an in-person conversation. Most adults have been schooled throughout life in how to interpret and engage in in-person conversations, but the data reveals a growing need to help Christians make the most of digital interactions: a "school of manners" for digital life, if you will.

Finally, the data leaves us with a sense that young people, in particular, are struggling to navigate the digital world—"digital Babylon," as David Kinnaman calls it. This world is rife with distractions, temptations, conflicting opinions (and "alternative facts"), tragedy and vehement disagreements. Not to mention cat videos! The digital world is, in many ways, unknown territory with few reliable maps available for guidance. It is a world in which young believers desperately need the Christian community to help them find their way.

Whether online or off, the experience of faith-sharing can run the gamut from exhilarating to disillusioning. Let's look at how spiritual conversations are perceived and experienced by the people who share and those with whom they share.

> Young believers desperately need the Christian community to help them find their way in "digital Babylon"

Q&A WITH RACHEL LEGOUTÉ

Rachel Legouté is the community manager for THRED, a project of Lutheran Hour Ministries. In that role, she publishes content on a variety of social media platforms and learns about their audience from the responses and conversations that follow. Rachel holds a degree in Christian outreach from Concordia University, and has a background in professional church work, not-for-profit management and corporate material analysis.

 Tell us about what THRED is trying to do and how it's going.

THRED is a digital outreach project that creates space online for an open and honest conversation about life, faith and Jesus with people of different backgrounds. More and more people are choosing online spaces to talk about topics they find relevant.

At THRED we strive to be a place where de-churched and non-churched people willingly come into contact with Christians to talk about real issues of our times. We believe that hearing other points of view is critical to developing dialogue that opens space for the gospel to be heard. We are encouraged by feedback from people who self-identify as agnostic or atheist, telling us how refreshing it is to share differing opinions in a place that challenges their thoughts without the conversation turning into a shouting match!

 While digital interactions are increasing, people still prefer in-person conversations about faith or religion. Given this, what do you think draws people to a digital space to have spiritual conversations?

People flock to social media and online forums to share their thoughts on just about *everything*. As people become more comfortable having conversations on digital platforms—about their kids, pets, dinner—it is natural for them to also have conversations about deeper subjects.

Spiritual conversations in a digital space are unique in that they happen at the pace of people's lives. Digital conversations don't typically happen in real time, meaning that people can consume a piece of content and then reflect on it and on their response, before posting a comment later. In the same way, they have time to digest comments they receive and drive the conversation forward at a pace that works with their schedule.

The low relational investment for beginner conversations can also foster a safe environment for easy sharing. For the most part, people in our spaces are complete strangers at first. They don't have a prior relationship. Some members of the THRED community express feeling free to be totally honest with their viewpoints from the get-go because they aren't worried about damaging an existing relationship.

While conversations that lead directly to a conversion experience are more likely to happen in person, we know that the road to faith is not always short or linear. We create a space that feels safe for people to share their ideas so that they're willing to come back for deeper conversations. As followers spend more time in our spaces, we see them open up more and more. We get to learn more of their life stories and gain a deeper understanding of how their life experiences shape their thoughts on life and faith.

? When you think about the conversations you've moderated on THRED, what can you say about people who are most effective at dialoging about faith? And what about those who are less effective—any common mishaps?

The hardest conversations to moderate on THRED are those involving Christians who are more interested in telling people what to think than in having a genuine dialogue. They may mean well, but in the name of "doctrine" these Christians are slowing down the journey of a non-Christian toward Jesus. That's why we try to model leading with a posture of listening. The question mark is a powerful piece of punctuation! We've seen many newcomers to our site completely disarmed by people who truly listen by asking them what they think and why they think it.

THERE ARE TWO SIDES TO EVERY CONVERSATION

DURING A SPIRITUAL CONVERSATION, PEOPLE REPORTED FEELING OR EXPERIENCING THE FOLLOWING:

● Christian ◐ Non-Christian

71% **40%**

PEACE

59% **53%**

LAUGHTER

55% **20%**

JOY

19% **8%**

EXHILARATION

11% **18%**

STRESS

6% **27%**

ANNOYANCE

6% **10%**

CONFUSION

4% **2%**

SHAME

3% **9%**

ANGER

46

INTIMACY MATTERS

 have had a big change in their life as a result of a spiritual conversation.

 of Christians say someone came to faith in Jesus after having a spiritual conversation with them.

 9 / 10 people who experienced a big life change as a result of a spiritual conversation say the conversation was with someone they know well or very well.

 7 / 10 people say that life change was a result of multiple conversations with one person (42%) or with more than one person (27%).

 of conversations that led to a big life change happened in person.

THE MAJORITY OF PEOPLE SAY THEY ARE GLAD THEY HAD THEIR MOST RECENT SPIRITUAL CONVERSATION

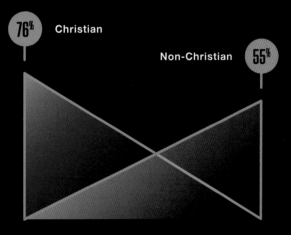

76% Christian

Non-Christian 55%

n=1,070 U.S. adults, June 22–July 13, 2017.

SPIRITUAL CONVERSATIONS FROM BOTH SIDES

3

"The happy life is social rather than solitary and conversationally deep rather than superficial," according to a study published in the journal *Psychological Science*. Researchers found that people who engage in more substantive conversations report higher measures of satisfaction and well-being than those who engage more frequently in small talk.[5]

For his most recent book, *Learning to Speak God from Scratch*, Barna worked with religion columnist Jonathan Merritt to interview U.S. adults for whom spiritual conversations are rare or nonexistent to find out why they don't talk more often about faith. Nearly three in 10 say the reason is that "religious conversations always seem to create tension or arguments" (28%).[6] (For more on people's reasons for not engaging in spiritual conversations, see pp. 53–55.)

This finding helps to explain why most people would choose to have a spiritual conversation with someone close to them: It just feels less risky to have a substantive, meaningful exchange on a tricky topic with someone you already know—and who already knows you.

Regardless of how they prioritize faith, most U.S. adults, Christian or not, prefer to talk about spiritual matters with close friends or family members rather than strangers or mere acquaintances. With the option to pick up to three people from a list of possibilities, a majority of practicing Christians (61%), non-practicing Christians (55%) and non-Christians (55%) choose "a friend" as the person they most want to talk with about faith.

Opting for "no one" on the list are one in five non-Christians (19%) and

Most U.S. adults prefer to talk about spiritual matters with close friends or family members

MY PREFERRED PARTNERS FOR SPIRITUAL CONVERSATIONS

% AMONG U.S. ADULTS; RESPONDENTS COULD CHOOSE UP TO THREE

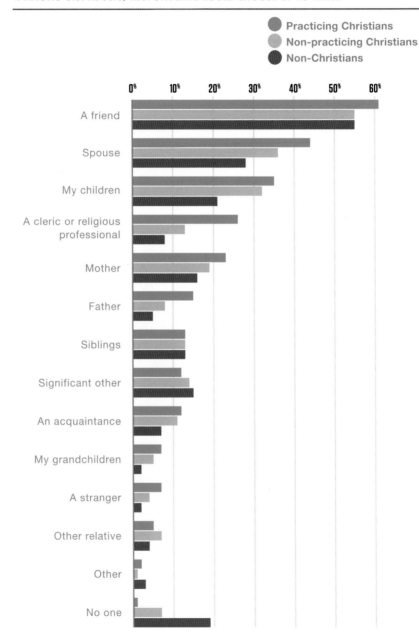

● Practicing Christians
● Non-practicing Christians
● Non-Christians

n=1,070 U.S. adults, June 22–July 13, 2017.

7 percent of non-practicing Christians. One-third or more of those who practice Christianity, on the other hand, say they like talking with their children (35%) or their spouse (44%) about faith, and one-quarter likes to talk with a pastor (26%) or their mother (23%).

Life stage has at least some impact here. For instance, Gen X and Boomers are much more likely than younger adults to choose their spouse (38% vs. 28% Millennials) or children (35% vs. 16%) in large part because they are much more likely to be married and to have kids. More young adults, on the other hand, choose "significant other" (23% vs. 11% older adults) because they are more inclined to be dating or cohabitating.

Fewer people in all faith categories put their father on the list, though Christians are twice as likely as non-Christians to do so (10% vs. 5%). Millennials, as the youngest adult generation, are therefore likelier than older adults to talk with either parent about faith—and more pick mom (35%) than choose dad (19%). At the same time, women across the board are more likely than men to choose "my children" (37% vs. 24%)—evidence that parent-child faith conversations are more often actually mother-child faith conversations. It also points to a reason adults are less apt to want to talk with their dad about faith: because fathers are less likely than mothers to have engaged with them on spiritual matters when they were young.

Parent-child faith conversations are more often actually mother-child faith conversations

These data reaffirm the need for churches to reach out specifically to men (who are less likely than women to attend church) and equip them with tools for talking about spiritual matters. As Barna found in new research among Gen Z, fathers play a key role in passing resilient faith on to their children; teens with parents who are engaged in Christian faith and practice are far more likely than other Christian young people to stay engaged in faith and practice.

Eager conversationalists are an exception—they are comparatively enthusiastic about talking faith with their kids (42%), even more than practicing Christians (35%) and much more than reluctant conversationalists (30%).

CONVERSATIONS THAT CHANGE LIVES

The goal of a spiritual conversation is not merely to pass on information or opinion but, hopefully, to transform lives. Is that what's happening? Are people having spiritual conversations that lead to lasting change? Many people are!

Given that the majority of Americans are having so few spiritual conversations, it may come as a surprise that a full one-third of all U.S. adults says they personally have made a "big change" in their life because of a conversation abwout faith (35%). Not surprisingly, Christians (41%) are more likely than non-Christians (17%) to say they have had a life-changing conversation.

As you might expect, these conversations are not coming out of the blue but are happening most often with people they know. Nine out of 10 of those who had a life-changing conversation say they had it with someone they know well (31%) or very well (57%). Again, this points to the profound influence we all have on those who are closest to us. There is much to be gained from pushing past our comfort zones with friends and family and bringing up the bigger issues of faith, God and the transcendent.

Of course, spiritual conversations are not always immediately fruitful. People often need to be exposed to ideas more than once before they begin to take root. Seven out of 10 people say their life change was actually a result of multiple conversations, either with just one person (42%) or with more than one person (27%).

How were those conversations conducted? In a variety of ways—but, again, in-person interactions top the list. Phone calls rank second place for all generations, but they are particularly common among Gen X. Millennials and Gen X are more likely than Boomers to use texting, instant messaging, video calling and emailing. These choices of media reflect the types of communication they are using more generally: Older generations are making more phone calls, younger generations are texting and tend to be more comfortable overall with digital communication. The larger point here is that these conversations can happen anywhere, on whatever form of communication one regularly uses. However, in-person conversations remain the most fruitful. Perhaps digital communications can serve as follow-up methods, after an in-person interaction, to help aid in the "multiple conversations" most people need in order to enact life change.

When it comes to the biggest life change of all, more than one-third of self-identified Christians says someone has come to believe in Jesus as Savior after they shared about their faith in him. As one might predict, eager

1 in 3 Christians says someone has come to believe in Jesus after they shared about their faith in him

People who don't talk very often about faith offer different reasons, but most of these fall into two broad categories: *avoidance* and *ambivalence.* For instance, among the top four responses given for not engaging in conversations are two that are avoidant: "Religious conversations always seem to create tension or arguments" (28%) and "I'm put off by how religion has been politicized" (17%). The other two responses indicate ambivalence: "I'm not religious and don't care about these kinds of topics" (23%) and "I don't feel like I know enough to talk about religious or spiritual topics" (17%). Here's the full list of options:

- Religious conversations always seem to create tension or arguments: **28%**
- I'm not religious and don't care about these kinds of topics: **23%**
- I'm put off by how religion has been politicized: **17%**
- I don't feel like I know enough to talk about religious or spiritual topics: **17%**
- I don't want to be known as a religious person: **7%**
- I don't know how to talk about religious or spiritual topics without sounding weird: **6%**
- I'm afraid people will see me as a fanatic or extremist: **5%**
- I'm embarrassed by the way religious language has been used in popular culture: **5%**
- I've been hurt by religious conversations in the past: **4%**
- Religious language and jargon feels cheesy or outdated: **4%**

Among all adults who rarely engage, Boomers are significantly more likely to say they are not religious and don't care about these kinds of topics (32% vs. 17% Millennials and Gen X, 22% Elders). Likewise, political liberals are more likely than conservatives to choose this option (28% vs. 15%). These groups tend more toward ambivalence or indifference than to frustration or fear.

Millennials, however, are much more likely to feel afraid that people will see them as a fanatic or extremist (10% vs. 3% Gen X, 4% Boomers, 1% Elders). This generation has grown up in a culture that values tolerance and freeing people to make their own decisions. One of the great

evils is to be perceived as bigoted. It makes sense that a fear of coming across as intolerant (often associated, as Millennials came of age, with religiosity) could turn them away from the topic altogether. Additionally, as we know from other research, young adults are more likely than any other age group to have friends who are different from them: different ethnicities, different religions, different social and political beliefs. They tend, therefore, to be more sensitive to offending other groups. They expect to live in a pluralistic society and so fear association with a group—fundamentalist Christians—that is often represented as opposed to ways of thinking or believing other than their own.

n=508 U.S. adults who never or rarely talk about their faith, May 15-19, 2017.

WHY DON'T YOU HAVE SPIRITUAL CONVERSATIONS MORE OFTEN?

Religious conversations always seem to create tension or arguments **28%**

29% This is the number-one reason Christians don't want to talk about faith

I'm not religious and don't care about these kinds of topics **23%**

55% This is the top reason people of no faith don't have spiritual conversations

Cannot recall / not sure **21%**

I'm put off by how religion has been politicized **17%**

I don't feel like I know enough to talk about religious or spiritual topics **17%**

I don't want to be known as a religious person **7%**

I don't know how to talk about religious or spiritual topics without sounding weird

I'm afraid people will see me as a fanatic or extremist 5%

10% This is especially true for Millennials

I'm embarrassed by the way religious language has been used in popular culture

I've been hurt by religious conversations in the past

13% Practicing Christians are the group most prone to blame this

Religious language and jargon feels cheesy or outdated

9% 1% Liberals are much more likely to say this than conservatives

n=522 | May 15-19, 2017 | from a Barna study conducted for the book *Learning to Speak God from Scratch* by Jonathan Merritt.

INTERACTIONS THAT LED TO MY BIG LIFE CHANGE

% AMONG U.S. ADULTS WHO EXPERIENCED A BIG CHANGE AFTER A SPIRITUAL CONVERSATION; RESPONDENTS COULD SELECT ALL THAT APPLY

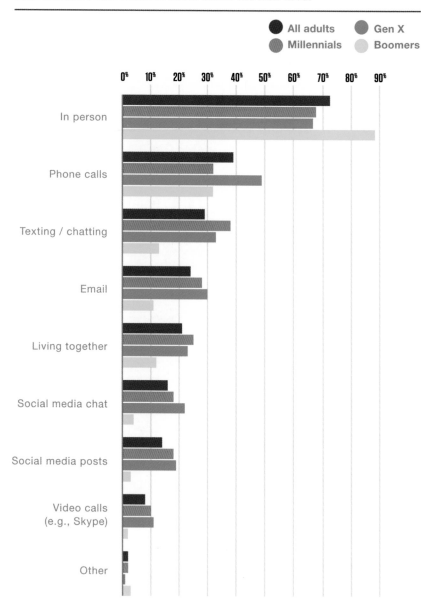

n=374 U.S. adults who report a big change after a spiritual conversation, June 22–July 13, 2017.

conversationalists, who shared their faith 10 or more times last year, are much more liable than those who share less often to say they have led someone to the Lord (47% vs. 34% reluctant). Perhaps less predictable is the fact that younger Christians are more likely than Boomers to say a conversation partner has committed their life to Christ after their talk about faith. Surprising as that may be, this finding squares with what younger and middle-aged Christians say about their responsibility to evangelize, which we touched on in chapter 1: Younger believers are more likely than their older sisters and brothers to agree that they personally have a responsibility to share their faith.

SOMEONE BELIEVED IN JESUS AS SAVIOR AFTER I TALKED WITH THEM ABOUT MY FAITH

% AMONG SELF-IDENTIFIED CHRISTIANS

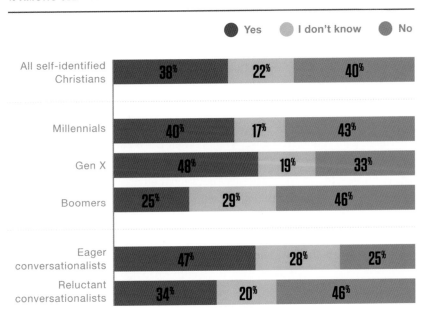

● Yes   ● I don't know   ● No

	Yes	I don't know	No
All self-identified Christians	38%	22%	40%
Millennials	40%	17%	43%
Gen X	48%	19%	33%
Boomers	25%	29%	46%
Eager conversationalists	47%	28%	25%
Reluctant conversationalists	34%	20%	46%

n=796 U.S. self-identified Christians, June 22–July 13, 2017.

THE BACK & FORTH OF SHARING FAITH

Barna asked U.S. adults who have had a spiritual conversation with someone who does not share their faith to recall details about that exchange. Researchers wanted to find out what, if anything, good conversations share in common. What is a good spiritual conversation? And who decides?

People can only fairly represent their own side of the conversation, but their individual experiences can nonetheless reveal differences between how various groups of people tend to approach and perceive the actual process of faith-sharing. For example, since most people express a preference for talking with a friend or family member about spiritual matters, we would expect that most would know the person with whom they had their latest spiritual conversation—and, in fact, eight out of 10 U.S. adults report knowing their conversation partner well (36%) or very well (42%).

There are differences, however, between Christians who share often, Christians who share infrequently and non-Christians—and between Christians of different generations. For example, compared to younger adults, more Boomers did not know their last spiritual conversation partner (24% vs. 16%). There's a reality here that's important to point out: Simply put, younger Christians are more likely to know (and be friends with) non-Christians. Whereas Boomer Christians are more likely to go outside their close friend group to find non-Christians, Millennial Christians are often surrounded by nonbelievers—because fewer Millennials overall identify as Christian.

Likewise, eager conversationalists are more likely not to have known the last person with whom they shared faith (22%) compared to 15 percent of reluctant conversationalists. On the other hand, eager conversationalists are also more willing and, well, eager to share their Christian faith with strangers or distant acquaintances. This may partly explain why eager conversationalists seem alert to cultural differences between their conversation partner and themselves—along with Millennials, who are a more diverse generation than older adults. These two groups of Christians are most likely to feel culturally different from their conversation partner, while Boomers are least likely (11% vs. 35% Millennials, 28% eager conversationalists). For Millennials this is partly a consequence of the more diverse cultural makeup of their generation. For eager conversationalists, this may reflect a priority on reaching across cultural divides to share the gospel.

Most Christians have faith discussions with people similar to them in age and cultural perspective—for example, fewer than half of Millennials say they talked with someone 10 or more years older (33%) or younger (15%). As we would expect, when it comes to those who *did* talk with someone from a different generation, younger adults are more likely to report a faith conversation with an older adult, and vice versa. (And, since non-Christians tend to skew younger, they talk more often with adults significantly older than younger—because there are just more older adults in the pool of potential conversationalists.)

Eager conversationalists are the exception to the "similar-to-me" rule: Six out of 10 report their conversation partner was either 10 years older (28%) or younger (31%) than themselves.

THE PERSON WITH WHOM I HAD MY MOST RECENT SPIRITUAL CONVERSATION

% AMONG U.S. ADULTS WHO HAVE HAD A CONVERSATION ABOUT THEIR FAITH WITH SOMEONE WHO DOES NOT SHARE THEIR FAITH

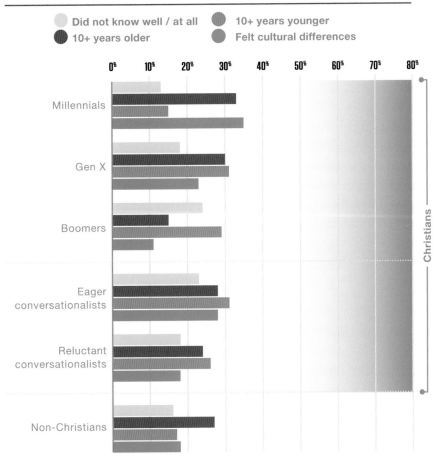

n=840 U.S. adults who have had a conversation about their faith, June 22–July 13, 2017.

Q&A WITH JEFFERSON BETHKE

Jefferson Bethke is the *New York Times* bestselling author of *Jesus > Religion* and *It's Not What You Think*, and coauthor with his wife, Alyssa, of *Love That Lasts*. Together they make YouTube videos and host a podcast about relationships and faith. They live in Maui with their daughter, Kinsley, and son, Kannon.

 What do you think the internet and social media offer people that's unique when it comes to exploring faith and talking about religion and spirituality?

What they offer is a double-edged sword. One of the blessings of digital spaces, and the internet cultures that form in those spaces, is being able to find answers to your questions and truth that moves you deeply. If you were an outsider in your community a hundred years ago, you didn't have many places to go where you could feel you belong. But digital spaces allow you to be a seeker on your own terms and find people who may be more loving and helpful than the people around you in physical space.

The downside, though, is too many people unwilling to stay put in communities where there are differences of opinion and perspective. That's not good. I think a willingness to stay put is very much one of the fortifying powers of spiritual growth. When there is a massive shift away from true community, face-to-face interaction and longstanding spiritual traditions—silence, communion, meditation on scripture, solitude, prayer, fasting, and so on—we're in trouble.

 At what point do you think the internet and social media fall short when it comes to spiritual conversations?

Digital spaces are great for starting a conversation, finding information and gaining understanding, but terrible for being truly known—and that's essential for any human walking healthily with the Lord. Being known requires genuine vulnerability, and generous acceptance when someone else is genuinely vulnerable, to lift the burden of shame that is heavy on so many of our friends and family. And vulnerability, in its truest and most beautiful form, just can't happen online.

When we asked who people are most comfortable having spiritual conversations with, fathers came out low on most people's lists. And when we asked fathers who they are comfortable having spiritual conversations with, we found they are not nearly as likely as mothers to say their kids. What do you think is happening here?

This is a crisis by all accounts. The practice and art of fatherhood is being lost day by day. There are a lot of factors, but I think one of the main reasons is that dads feel incompetent in this area, and most guys—and some women too, of course, but it's a sharper pain point for many men—can't stand the feeling of incompetence. When we feel like a failure, shame beckons. Then we retreat inside ourselves and close off all vulnerability in a failing effort to protect ourselves from shame. This loop repeats itself over and over again.

Most dads I know are great about talking in depth when it comes to work, sports or opinions on current events, because those are areas where we are expected to be experts. But when it comes to our children's hearts, and pursuing them on an emotional level, we think of that as the mom's job, the pastor's job, the teacher's job—when, in reality, one of the primary callings of a dad isn't to work, to provide, but to capture his child's heart. That can only happen when we lead with vulnerability. Transparency and intimacy beget more transparency and intimacy.

Time is a huge factor. According to research I've seen recently, the number of hours a father spends at home keeps shrinking. Dads have fewer and fewer touch-points throughout the day to build relationship and intimacy with our kids. I'm not saying that staying home or working from home should be the goal for every dad, but I do think it's important to get some perspective on what we gain and what we lose by being away so much. Is it possible we're in the Matrix and don't even realize it, serving the economy instead of our family?

Much of this points to a general lack of conversation and relationship between generations. In another Barna study, nearly seven in 10 among each generation said their close friends are mostly similar to them in life stage. The Church is one of few remaining modern institutions with the capacity and opportunity to create enriching relationships between members of different generations.

MY MOST RECENT SPIRITUAL CONVERSATION, PART 1

% AMONG U.S. ADULTS WHO HAVE HAD A CONVERSATION ABOUT THEIR FAITH WITH SOMEONE WHO DOES NOT SHARE THEIR FAITH

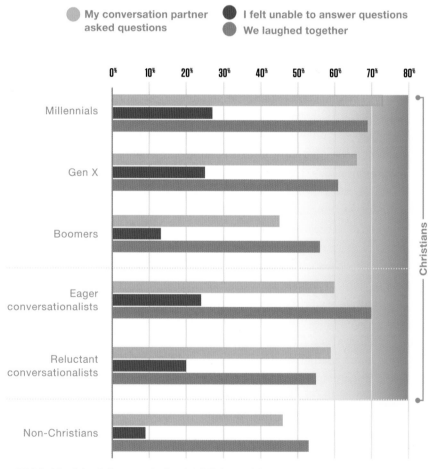

● My conversation partner asked questions

● I felt unable to answer questions

● We laughed together

n=840 U.S. adults who have had a conversation about their faith, June 22–July 13, 2017.

So what do most spiritual conversations have in common? Laughter, for one thing! A majority of all U.S. adults who engaged in a faith conversation says they laughed with their conversation partner (58%). Questions are also a common component: Most Christians (59%) and a plurality of non-Christians (46%; 16% don't know) say the other person asked questions during

MY MOST RECENT SPIRITUAL CONVERSATION, PART 2

% AMONG U.S. ADULTS WHO HAVE HAD A CONVERSATION ABOUT THEIR FAITH WITH SOMEONE WHO DOES NOT SHARE THEIR FAITH

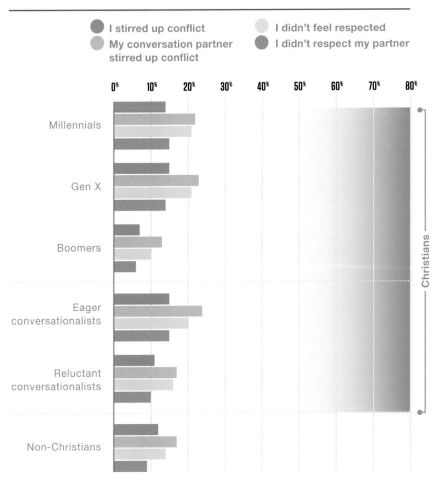

- I stirred up conflict
- My conversation partner stirred up conflict
- I didn't feel respected
- I didn't respect my partner

n=840 U.S. adults who have had a conversation about their faith, June 22–July 13, 2017.

their conversation—and they were questions most respondents felt equipped to answer.

Further reflecting on the experience, however, some people don't feel wholly positive. Younger Christians are more likely than older ones to report some negative experiences in their conversations. Eager conversationalists, especially, say their conversation partner stirred up conflict. (In fact *all* Christians are more likely to say the other person instigated conflict than to say they did so themselves, indicating they have a tendency to see the other as aggressive.)

I AM GLAD ABOUT MY LATEST SPIRITUAL CONVERSATION

% AMONG U.S. ADULTS WHO HAVE HAD A CONVERSATION ABOUT THEIR FAITH WITH SOMEONE WHO DOES NOT SHARE THEIR FAITH

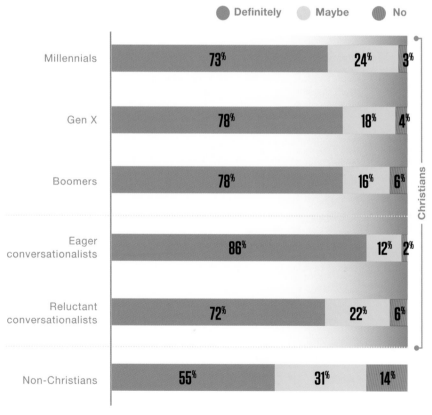

Legend: ● Definitely ● Maybe ● No

	Definitely	Maybe	No
Millennials	73%	24%	3%
Gen X	78%	18%	4%
Boomers	78%	16%	6%
Eager conversationalists	86%	12%	2%
Reluctant conversationalists	72%	22%	6%
Non-Christians	55%	31%	14%

(Millennials through Reluctant conversationalists are grouped as Christians)

n=840 U.S. adults who have had a conversation about their faith, June 22–July 13, 2017.

There are probably a few things going on here. Eager conversationalists (and young Christians) are the groups most likely to have spiritual conversations in the first place. As a result, they are probably having more of a variety of conversations, both positive and negative. Eager conversationalists, in turn, seem to be less put off by the negative aspects of these conversations—or, at least, negative conversations do not appear to dampen their enthusiasm for having more of them.

Yet these negative factors do not guarantee a bad outcome. Reflecting on their most recent conversation about faith, nearly three-quarters of all U.S. adults say they are glad about having had the discussion (72%)—but those who are *not* glad tend to be non-Christians (14% vs. 5% self-identified Christians). A mellow conversation, in which there is little or no conflict or unpleasant feelings, is not necessarily a conversation. In fact, when analyzing what makes a person likely to be glad about having had the conversation—accounting for conflict, respect, laughing together, how well they knew the conversation partner, whether they felt unable to answer a question, age gaps, and whether the other person asked questions—researchers found that conflict does not play a significant role in how people feel after the conversation.

Accounting for all of the various factors included in this study, those most likely to be happy with their conversation are eager conversationalists who knew their conversation partner very well—highlighting both their confidence in the subject matter and comfort in the relationship.

Negative conversations do not appear to dampen the enthusiasm of eager conversationalists

FAITH-SHARING & FEELINGS

"I almost never speak of my faith but when I do it feels wonderful!" wrote one Christian woman in answer to an open-ended question. Many other Christians experience similarly positive emotions, including peace (71%), joy (55%) and even exhilaration (19%). These feelings are especially concentrated among eager conversationalists, who share their faith often, but less so among those who share infrequently. Most eager conversationalists genuinely enjoy talking with others about their faith—and the fact that they are just as likely to experience negative feelings indicates that many of them are willing to push through their own discomfort in order to engage.

The experience seems to be different for non-Christians, however. A plurality reports feeling peace (40%), but the second most common emotion after a spiritual conversation is annoyance (27%). In fact, they are more likely than Christians to report feeling both annoyance and anger. This makes sense: Non-Christians do not spend comparable energy thinking about religion or

EMOTIONS I EXPERIENCE WHEN I TALK ABOUT FAITH

% AMONG U.S. ADULTS WHO HAVE HAD A CONVERSATION ABOUT THEIR FAITH

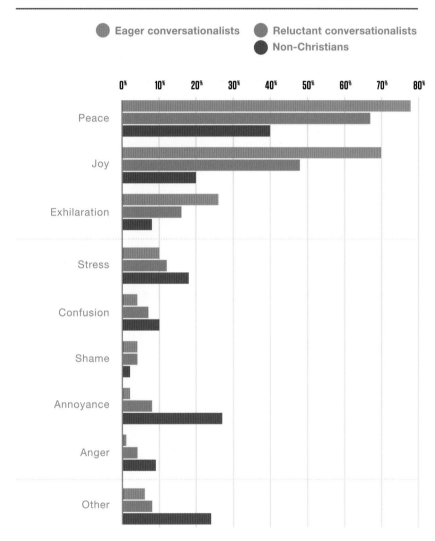

n≈840 U.S. adults who have had a conversation about their faith, June 22–July 13, 2017.

faith and are thus less likely to be comfortable or happy to delve into these topics of conversation. And, for some non-Christians—especially established atheists or agnostics—such conversations may open old wounds or stir up antagonism around a topic they have already decided on. Christians, then, must enter into such conversations with gentleness and grace. And, as frequently seen in this report, such conversations seem to be most effective when both parties know each other well.

Of course, a true spiritual conversation will not always (or even often) be fully positive. These conversations touch on some of the deepest anxieties and questions people wrestle with; they will inevitably stir up tension of some kind. One takeaway for spiritual leaders here is the need to train and empower Christians in navigating tense topics and even conflict during conversations about faith.

In the next chapter, we take a look at eager conversationalists—to find out more about what makes this group uniquely equipped and willing to engage in spiritual conversations.

Spiritual conversations touch on some of the deepest anxieties and questions people wrestle with

Q&A WITH DANA BYERS

Dana Byers is a pioneer in the online church movement. She began as a Life.Church Online volunteer in 2006. The next year, Dana and her young family sold nearly everything they owned to fund living overseas to launch BlueDoor Ministries, Inc. The first online church planters in history, the Byers family's purpose was to help pastors launch online churches outside the U.S. in a variety of languages and to expand the reach of Life. Church Online. After moving back to the States, Dana wrote "The Art of Online Ministry" and became Associate Online Campus Pastor at Life. Church. Today she is Executive Pastor of Mercy Road Church in Carmel, Indiana.

In your years of planting online churches, what have you found are the components of meaningful, even transformative, virtual spiritual conversations?

A core element of positive online interactions is developing the ability to be nearly unoffendable. A lot of people who've been hurt by the church are happy to let others know about it on social media. So when someone has arms flailing and fists flying in their responses, your best approach is not to respond the way they are expecting: negatively. Let them be mad. Admit they could get hurt again by a church, or in any other organization, because it's comprised of imperfect humans. Then invite them to give this Jesus thing another shot.

Your focus doesn't need to be converting people to follow Jesus; God works on people's hearts. You can simply focus on representing Christ well: Listen, show genuine concern, pray as the interaction is happening so you can hear from the Holy Spirit what your next step should be.

Lead people as far as they're willing to go. Be cognizant of the fact that online interactions are often incredible launching pads. Be an entrepreneurial online evangelist by always identifying a next step. Invite them to meet for coffee if they're local. Connect them to a local church if you know a good one in their part of the world. Get them to visit your online or face-to-face small group. Offer to pray with them and email to check in next week.

? Do you think it's possible to have good spiritual conversations on social media? And if so, how?

It's absolutely possible. I've seen it happen more times than I can count. However, the most difficult spiritual conversations online are with people who have a point to prove. Sadly, many non-Christians in the U.S. and beyond have had experiences with Christians who have something to prove—and have already decided they don't want any part of it. For good conversations to happen online and elsewhere, here are some practical steps to take:

- **Approach spiritual conversations with a non-competitive, everyone's-welcome-at-the-table mindset.** This lowers participants' guard and represents Christ as we know Him to be: full of both grace and truth. Judgmental, assumptive or exclusionary language is as damaging on social media as it is in person.
- **Consider your face-to-face spiritual conversations for comparison's sake.** Do you pummel the other person with statistics, churchy language and guilt-ridden comments? Do you cram Bible verses down their throat? Probably not. The same guide-lines should be followed online.
- **Think the best of the other person.** There's a good chance they're hurting or have a skewed image of Christ-followers. They might merely be curious in their question, or they may be in the middle of what's been a long and painful spiritual journey. You cannot know all the details, so receive whatever they offer and respond graciously.
- **Invest a little time in studying the individual's online presence to develop your empathy toward them.** What do others say on their Facebook wall? Does this person share photos on Twitter? What do they do for a living? You don't need to become an expert on the individual, but you can get a glimpse into the life of this person whom God created and loves so much that he put you in their path to point them to him.

What are some good rules of the virtual road for Christians who want to share their faith online?

Determine *why* you want to minister online before you determine *how* you'll do it. Every ounce of energy you pour into online outreach is worthwhile, but no one wants another online church or social media missionary that is focused on increasing tithes, adding to their attendance or making a name for themselves.

Recognize that online ministry is legitimate. I think there's a tendency for us to undermine the capacity for life change to happen online, and we sometimes forget that God's not bound by time, space or the internet. He works through every medium we invite him into. Taking seriously the time you're online to minister is a key component of making a Kingdom impact with your life.

Recognize the responsibility online ministry carries with it. You will get middle-of-the-night Facebook messages from suicidal people. You will be tempted to take it personally when someone curses God. You will doubt that you're making a difference.

Authenticity should be the norm. No one will be impressed by you having all the answers. Honesty adds a depth and richness to the quality of interactions you can have online, second only to surrounding your conversations with prayer.

Speaking of prayer: pray continually. Online ministry always, always, always involves prayer. If anyone comes to a physical church to minister without having been in prayer, they are unprepared. The same goes for online ministry: If you or I show up without inviting God into the equation, we're not equipped and could do more damage than good.

Understand your role. You aren't called to be the savior of someone's life. You are called to be open and available to be used by God in the online interaction. Sometimes people don't respond or come back. That's on them. You simply need to be faithful to meeting them where they're at.

EAGER TO SHARE

4

As we've seen throughout this report, Christians who talk about their faith a lot are different in their behaviors and perceptions from those who don't. Through analysis, it became clear to researchers that getting to know these eager conversationalists could be helpful for church and ministry leaders, who are called to equip Christians to live and proclaim the good news. What is happening with these sisters and brothers that makes them so eager to share? Who are the one in four Christians who talk about faith 10 or more times a year (27%)?

Demographically, it doesn't appear that gender, ethnicity or age cohort makes a significant impact on faith-sharing frequency—and that's worth noting, especially when it comes to age. The Christian community rightly worries about the church dropout problem among Millennials, so it's great news that young adults who remain active in the faith are, statistically speaking, just as eager as older Christians to share: 24 percent are eager conversationalists, compared to 27 percent of older adults (a difference that is within the margin of error).

The demographic difference that appears to make a difference is having kids; being a parent correlates to more faith conversations. Three in 10 Christians who have children are eager conversationalists (29%), compared to one in five of those who don't (21%). Most parents choose to raise their children in their own faith tradition, so it makes sense that they would talk more frequently about spiritual matters than those not engaged at home in passing on Christian faith to the next generation. In Barna's recent research among

Gen Z 13- to 18-year-olds, teens with parents who are engaged Christians—they make faith a priority on a variety of measures—are much more likely to themselves be engaged in faith. In other words, parents who are eager to talk with their kids about spiritual matters raise kids who are likewise eager. This signals the importance of faith-sharing from generation to generation. While we may often think of sharing faith as something that is done with strangers or with those who are non-Christians, some of the most significant and impactful conversations we can have are at home. Children who grow up regularly talking about faith and seeing their parents integrate faith into everyday life are much more likely to continue being actively engaged in their faith as they grow older.

SPIRITUAL PRACTICES & DEEP COMMITMENT

Faith tradition, Christian practice and the priority people assign to their faith also make a difference. As you might expect, those who engage in various faith practices in their own life are also the ones who are most likely to talk about their faith with others. This makes sense: If you are regularly thinking about your faith, connecting it to your daily life and seeking God's will in your activities, then spiritual matters are on your mind more often. In turn, such thoughts make their way into your conversations with others.

EAGER VS. RELUCTANT: ENGAGEMENT IN SPIRITUAL PRACTICES DURING THE PAST WEEK

% *AMONG U.S. SELF-IDENTIFIED CHRISTIANS*

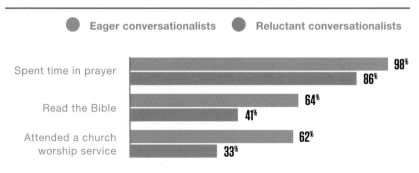

● Eager conversationalists ● Reluctant conversationalists

Spent time in prayer — 98%, 86%
Read the Bible — 64%, 41%
Attended a church worship service — 62%, 33%

n=796 U.S. self-identified Christians, June 22–July 13, 2017.

Nearly all eager conversationalists say they are "personally committed to Jesus Christ" (97% vs. 86% reluctant), and regular church attendance, Bible reading and prayer are common practices among this group. One-third of Christians who attend church at least once a month are eager conversationalists (36%), but only 13 percent of "unchurched" Christians—those who do not regularly attend—share their faith frequently. Looked at another way, 62 percent of those who are eager were in church last Sunday, compared to one-third of those who are reluctant (33%). Likewise, eager conversationalists are more likely than those who are reluctant to have read the Scriptures (64% vs. 41%) and spent time in prayer (98% vs. 86%) during the past week.

A strong priority on faith is another characteristic of an eager conversationalist. Eight out of 10 eager conversationalists strongly agree that "your religious faith is very important in your life today" (82%), yet just half of reluctant conversationalists strongly agree (48%). Relatedly, those who regularly attend church *and* say their faith is very important in their lives (Barna calls them "practicing Christians") are more likely to be eager: 42 percent share often, compared to only 15 percent of non-practicing Christians. When it comes to Christian tradition, Protestants are more inclined than Catholics to share faith frequently: Half of practicing Protestants (50%) and three in 10 practicing Catholics (30%) qualify as eager.

Beliefs seem to be at least as influential as faith practice on how often Christians share their faith—perhaps even more influential than regular church attendance. Eager conversationalists are more likely than reluctant conversationalists to subscribe to orthodox Christian beliefs about God and

1 in 3 Christians who regularly attend church is an eager conversationalist

EAGER VS. RELUCTANT: BELIEFS

% STRONGLY AGREE AMONG U.S. SELF-IDENTIFIED CHRISTIANS

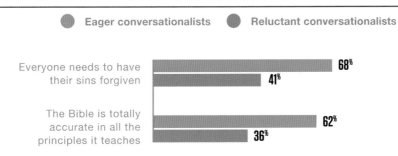

● Eager conversationalists   ● Reluctant conversationalists

Everyone needs to have their sins forgiven — 68% / 41%

The Bible is totally accurate in all the principles it teaches — 62% / 36%

n=796 U.S. self-identified Christians, June 22–July 13, 2017.

the Bible. They are nearly twice as likely to strongly agree that "the Bible is totally accurate in all of the principles that it teaches" (62% vs. 36% reluctant) and two-thirds strongly agree that "everyone needs to have their sins forgiven" (68% vs. 41%).

Perhaps not surprisingly, there appears to be a relationship between a Christian's understanding of the afterlife and the frequency with which she talks about her faith. Based on answers to a question about what will happen to them after they die, researchers grouped believers into three "afterlife groups" to examine possible correlations. Just over half belong to the "orthodox" group, which agrees with the doctrinal statement, "When you die you will go to heaven because you have confessed your sins and have accepted Jesus Christ as your Savior" (53%). About one-quarter fall into the "moralist" group (22%); these Christians view heaven as something to be earned through maximum human effort. The "universalist" group is made up of only 5 percent of Christians, but their agreement with the statement "when you die you will go to heaven because God loves all people and will not let them perish" strongly correlates with fewer reported spiritual conversations.

Two-thirds of eager conversationalists have an orthodox understanding of life after death (64%), while only 49 percent of reluctant conversationalists

There is greater evangelistic urgency associated with an orthodox view of life after death

EAGER VS. RELUCTANT: LIFE AFTER DEATH

% AMONG U.S. SELF-IDENTIFIED CHRISTIANS

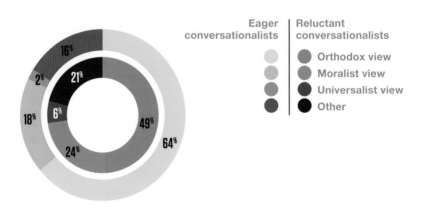

Eager conversationalists | Reluctant conversationalists

- Orthodox view
- Moralist view
- Universalist view
- Other

n=796 U.S. self-identified Christians, June 22–July 13, 2017.

adhere to the orthodox view. Just 10 percent of the universalist group have frequent conversations about faith.

What's going on here? It's likely there is greater evangelistic urgency associated with an orthodox view of what happens after death.

PERSONAL RESPONSIBILITY & CONFIDENCE

When describing evangelism, one Christian wrote of her approach, "My 'job' is to allow the Holy Spirit to speak through me. My own testimony and a few words from Scripture are powerful. The Holy Spirit works on their heart."

Another focused on his actions rather than his words: "All of my daily activities revolve around my response to the free gift of my salvation through Jesus. That is what drives my life every day."

For many eager conversationalists, this drive is energized by personal experience: Six in 10 say they have made a big change in their life as a result of a conversation about faith (59%), nearly twice as many as those who share less frequently (34%). Perhaps consequently, three-quarters of eager conversationalists agree they have a personal responsibility to share their faith, compared to half of reluctant conversationalists (77% vs. 49%)—and when it comes to the ways they approach spiritual conversations, many who often share have an "all of the above" style. From Facebook, to email, to in-person conversations, a majority of them reports using more than half of the available options, compared to only two methods selected by a majority of those who had fewer than 10 conversations last year. Christians eager to share their faith are more willing to use any of the approaches Barna examined. They seem to be more flexible and creative and appear more comfortable with faith-sharing all the way around. It's likely they even customize their approach to different kinds of people. It's also more likely that they are filtering all of their interactions through a lens of faith—whether that's online or in person.

Confidence may have something to do with the disparity between these two groups. Two-thirds of eager conversationalists say they definitely "feel qualified to share my faith" (65%) but only 40 percent of reluctant conversationalists say so—the same percentage that says they maybe feel that way (vs. 31% eager). As we saw in chapter 1, eager Christians are also more likely to say they actively seek or create opportunities to share their faith (27% vs. 15%).

> Christians eager to share their faith appear to be more flexible and creative in their approach

WHAT MAKES FOR AN EAGER CONVERSATIONALIST?

Believe they have a personal responsibility to share their faith with non-believers — **77%**

Have personally experienced a big change in their life due to a conversation about faith — **53%**

Believe God needs Christians to be consistently involved in evangelism in order to convert non-Christians — **68%**

Believe everyone needs their sins forgiven, and forgiveness of sins is only through Jesus' death and resurrection — **90%**

Believe when they die they will go to heaven because they have confessed their sins and trust in Jesus as Savior — **64%**

Say faith is very important in their life today — **98%**

Have prayed in the past week — **98%**

Have read the Bible in the past week — **64%**

Have attended church in the past week — **62%**

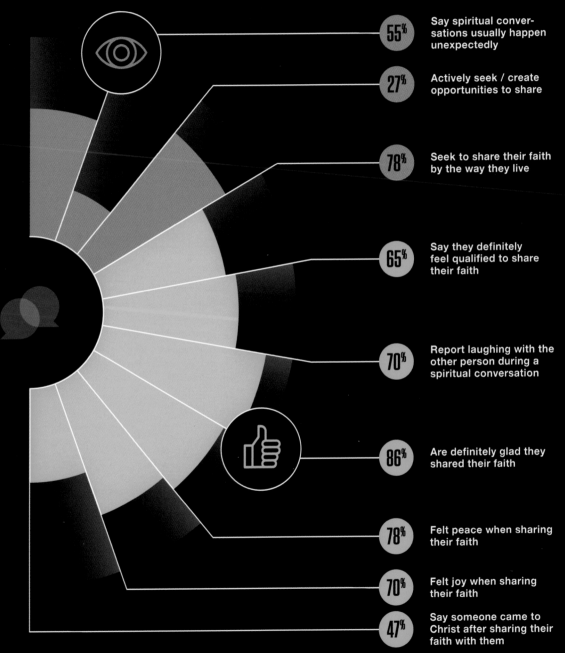

A sense of personal responsibility

Belief in salvation through Jesus alone

Good spiritual practices

Intentionality & readiness

Confidence coupled with positive experiences

55% Say spiritual conversations usually happen unexpectedly

27% Actively seek / create opportunities to share

78% Seek to share their faith by the way they live

65% Say they definitely feel qualified to share their faith

70% Report laughing with the other person during a spiritual conversation

86% Are definitely glad they shared their faith

78% Felt peace when sharing their faith

70% Felt joy when sharing their faith

47% Say someone came to Christ after sharing their faith with them

n=191 U.S. self-identified Christians who qualify as eager conversationalists.

EAGER VS. RELUCTANT: APPROACHES TO FAITH-SHARING

% AMONG U.S. SELF-IDENTIFIED CHRISTIANS, RESPONDENTS COULD SELECT ALL THAT APPLY

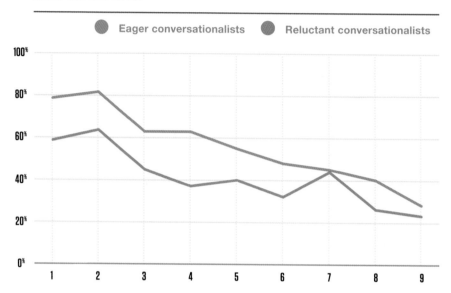

● Eager conversationalists   ● Reluctant conversationalists

1. Share by the way you live, rather than by words
2. Ask questions about their beliefs and life experiences
3. Tell the other person about the changes and benefits of life in Christ
4. Spend time praying for the person and your time together before you get together
5. Tell them the story of how you first came to believe in Jesus

6. Quote passages from the Bible
7. Use the same basic approach every time you share your faith
8. Send something digitally
9. Challenge them to defend their lifestyle or beliefs in view of your beliefs and convictions

n=796 U.S. self-identified Christians, June 22–July 13, 2017.

It's possible this is related to a perception of adequate preparation: One-third of frequent sharers strongly agrees their church does a good job training people to be effective evangelists (32%), compared to one-quarter of those who share less often (23%). While practice begets confidence—the more often you have spiritual conversations, the more comfortable you are with having them—this also points to an opportunity for churches to provide more training for Christians who struggle to feel comfortable talking about their faith.

EAGER VS. RELUCTANT: I FEEL QUALIFIED TO SHARE MY FAITH

% AMONG U.S. SELF-IDENTIFIED CHRISTIANS

● Definitely   ● Maybe   ● No

Eager conversationalists: 65% | 31% | 4%

Reluctant conversationalists: 40% | 40% | 20%

n=796 U.S. self-identified Christians, June 22–July 13, 2017.

Of course, it's also possible that some eager conversationalists generally have a more extroverted temperament or strongly held opinions than some who are reluctant. When Barna asked about a variety of topics other than faith, researchers found that eager conversationalists are more likely to have engaged in conversations about health (80% vs. 71% reluctant), politics (77% vs. 68%), parenting (69% vs. 55%) and LGBTQ issues (55% vs. 41%). Whatever the reason, frequent sharers seem to be more open overall and certainly more interested in turning ordinary encounters into spiritual conversations. They are people for whom spiritual conversations come naturally and often in the course of everyday life. This, coupled with their feeling of being qualified to share, leads them not to shy away from spiritual topics.

This is significant for ministry leaders: How can you equip laypeople to feel ready for these kinds of conversations? How can you help them understand the ways God is at work in everyday situations?

Similar to their any-and-all ethos when it comes to approach, eager conversationalists tend to use many means of communication to engage in conversations about faith (see the chart below). On a related question, one-quarter strongly agrees that "tech and digital interactions have changed how I share my faith" (28%), compared to just 15 percent of reluctant conversationalists. This also signals a willingness (and confidence) to adjust their sharing styles for the person and medium.

What can we take away from these commonalities and characteristics of eager conversationalists?

> For those who share faith often, spiritual conversations come naturally in the course of everyday life

EAGER VS. RELUCTANT: ENGAGEMENT IN FAITH-SHARING

% AMONG SELF-IDENTIFIED CHRISTIANS, RESPONDENTS COULD SELECT ALL THAT APPLY

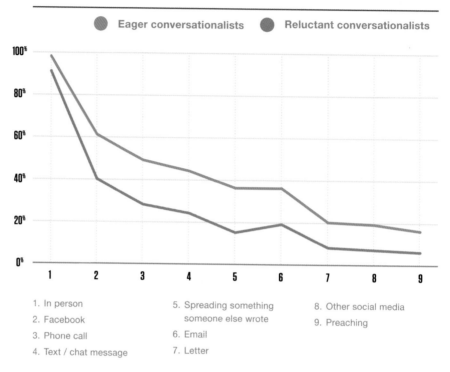

● Eager conversationalists   ● Reluctant conversationalists

1. In person
2. Facebook
3. Phone call
4. Text / chat message
5. Spreading something someone else wrote
6. Email
7. Letter
8. Other social media
9. Preaching

n=796 U.S. self-identified Christians, June 22–July 13, 2017.

One of the clearest takeaways is a simple one: The more people think about faith, the more they talk about it. Eager conversationalists are actively engaged in their faith on a daily and weekly basis: They are reading the Bible, praying often, attending church regularly. Such activities undoubtedly produce fruit in their lives and center their activities and interactions around their faith. God is on their mind—and such thoughts spill out into their conversations, as well.

This should encourage church leaders! Discipling believers to engage with God more often through scripture, prayer and regular church attendance is the bread and butter of church. And such activities do, in fact, produce disciples who take their faith out into the world.

In the final section, we look more closely at the implications of this full report—and how to apply these findings in day-to-day life and ministry.

Q&A WITH MICAH GLENN

Rev. Micah Glenn is the executive director of Lutheran Hope Center in Ferguson, Missouri. He is married to Deaconess Dorothy Glenn and they have three children: Jonathan (4), Talitha (2) and David (1).

 People today are hesitant to share beliefs or talk about faith because they are afraid of the conflict it might stir up. What do you see as the main challenges and opportunities for sharing faith in a tense political climate?

The first challenge for sharing faith in our political environment is how generalized and polarized these discussions become. If you're pro-life you get labeled a woman-hater. If you believe in social programming for the underserved, then you're an America-hating communist. This naturally prevents any worthwhile dialogue from taking place.

I also think people have a great fear of being exposed on mass level through social media. It's difficult to have a private conversation with someone in public, when an eavesdropper can screenshot or video your conversation, put it on Twitter or Facebook and a few million people can see what you said in a matter of a couple days—and these platforms easily skew the context of what was said.

But the greatest challenge I find is that people sometimes let their political party dictate where they fall on faith topics of a social nature. Even if their confession of faith contradicts their political party, they are afraid of what their political comrades will think if they disagree on certain issues.

 We were surprised to find that Millennials express more interest in spiritual conversations than older Americans. In your experience, what are the differences between spiritual conversations you have with youth and those you've had with adults?

Most of the conversations I have with youth are focused on how the word of God applies to their everyday life in response to what they see in the world. Youth I know want to be able to translate biblical themes into their different vocational contexts: school, work, friendships and so on. They want to know how to behave in a Christian manner toward people, especially people that are different from them, and so many of our spiritual conversations focus on love and compassion. They're also thirsty for answers about the pain and suffering in the world. In all of these things, simple one-word answers—like saying it's because of sin or the Fall—are unacceptable. You have to be willing to dig deeply into these conversation.

The conversations I have with older adults lean toward apologetics. Youth care about apologetics, but in my experience not nearly as much as their parents do. These conversations take many forms, but usually they move in a direction of examining the problem then applying an answer, whether the answer requires further research or they already have the solution at hand. Conversations with older adults are also tinged with concerns about legacy. They want the next generation to be passionate about the things they think are most important, so that faith will be passed on from generation to generation.

 You work in a culturally and ethnically diverse area. Do you notice unique characteristics in how different communities approach spiritual conversations and topics?

In my experience, white Christians tend to be far more worried than black Christians about offending someone, especially a person they don't know, in a faith conversation. Of course outliers exist in both ethnic groups, but more often than not when I'm having a conversation with a black person, there just aren't any taboo topics.

Other great differences are between socioeconomic groups. It can be difficult and somewhat insensitive to talk to someone about the eternal prosperity to come when Jesus returns when the person you're talking to is worried about where they will sleep or what they are going to eat. For those of us who are well fed and fairly paid with benefits, the future glory of God's kingdom is something we can easily look forward to. It is more than possible, of course, to experience joy and peace even when one's basic needs aren't met, but those of us who don't struggle to make ends meet should be humble and sensitive about how we challenge those who do.

WORTH TALKING ABOUT

There is much to unpack in this study and plenty of implications for how we can encourage more and better spiritual conversations. But perhaps the most potent finding is this:

THE LESS PEOPLE THINK ABOUT GOD, THE LESS THEY TALK ABOUT GOD.

And, simply put, people are thinking about God less and less.

The decline in spiritual conversations evident in this report tracks with an overall decline in religious belief and practice in America, which Barna has studied for more than three decades.

It may sound dire, but there is also good news: The *more* people think about God, the more they want to talk about God, about their beliefs and about their faith experiences. Active and engaged Christians remain eager to discuss spiritual matters, even as society around them grows increasingly reluctant to do so.

Church leaders: If you want to increase the number of spiritual conversations your church is having, focus on intentionally developing a rhythm between spiritual conversations and spiritual practices.

It is good news that spiritual conversations are a natural byproduct of spiritual practices. When a nominal Christian is transformed into an active disciple, they start talking. People whose lives are changed by God and who

> If you want to increase the number of spiritual conversations your church is having, focus on spiritual practices

daily interact with him are excited to share their hope with others. This can make them incredibly powerful witnesses in a time when transcendent hope seems hard to come by.

This brings to mind some familiar verses that Christians often reference when talking about faith conversations: "If someone asks about your hope as a believer, always be ready to explain it. But do this in a gentle and respectful way" (1 Peter 3:15–16).

We tend to focus our reading of this command on the word *explain* instead of on the word *ask*. We prioritize giving would-be evangelists information to help them accurately and clearly explain Christian doctrine, rather than equipping them as hope-filled disciples to be gentle and respectful. In our always-connected culture, however, information is cheap. Hope, on the other hand, is a hard-to-find treasure.

With that in mind, maybe we should give a greater part of our attention to living more deeply into Christian hope. Perhaps more people would ask us about it, and we'd be more eager to tell them about it when they do.

Let's use the rest of this space to look at what it takes to help Christians feel eager and ready—how to overcome the obstacles of today's world and to embrace its opportunities. Our hope is that, as you talk and pray through these challenges with your team, you will formulate a guidebook of sorts for helping Christians have meaningful faith conversations that fits your context and community.

PAY & DRAW ATTENTION TO THE SPIRITUAL DIMENSION OF LIFE

In a recently rediscovered essay first published in 1946, C. S. Lewis celebrates Europe's move away from paganism to modernity, "from the old fear, the old reverence, the old restraints" to "a universe of colourless electrons . . . which is presently going to run down and annihilate all organic life everywhere and forever."[7] (That's British humor—er, humour.)

The budding disenchantment Lewis identified in the wake of WWII is now in full bloom. Science explains life, and busyness—work, entertainment, always-on technology—fills it up. Time for contemplation and concern for anything nonmaterial seems pointless to many people. This includes self-identified Christians; only 57 percent strongly agree their faith is very important to their life. Relatedly, the reason most non-Christians don't have spiritual conversations boils down to this: They just aren't interested. (Many Christians know it—nearly half say non-Christians don't have any interest in hearing about Jesus.)

And, as David Kinnaman reported in *You Lost Me*, many Millennials say they dropped out of church involvement because it no longer felt personally relevant to them. What they did on Sunday morning seemed disconnected from the rest of their lives. For many, their church experience neither equipped them to grapple honestly with the materialist culture "out there," nor helped them "re-enchant" the everyday, infusing the secular with the sacred.

Christians (especially those who are not yet prioritizing their faith) need help making meaningful connections between everyday life and the life of the spirit—both for themselves and their would-be conversation partners. How can your faith community help Christians follow Jesus with their *whole* lives and then tell their story in a way that makes sense in a culture less and less attuned to the spiritual dimension of human life and relationships?

> Christians need help making meaningful connections between everyday life and the life of the spirit

BE A FAITHFUL FRIEND

The vast majority of spiritual conversations, including those that lead to transformative life change, happen face to face with a friend or family member. Yes, mobile technology is a growing part of many people's lives—but it's not at all clear that this is for the best. In fact, researcher Jean Twenge makes a compelling case that teen anxiety and depression have skyrocketed in tandem with widespread adoption of the smartphone.[8] We may have more ways to communicate than ever before, but they don't appear to be much help when it comes to cultivating intimacy and connectedness with others—at least, not on their own.

Psychologist Robin Dunbar has compiled persuasive evidence that human beings are cognitively capable of participating in a social network of about 150 acquaintances ("Dunbar's number").[9] Those aren't close friendships; according to Dunbar, most of us can only maintain between 5 and 15 intimate relationships—that is, the friends and family members with whom we can share most thoughts and feelings, and they still like us. These close relationships are very often where rich spiritual conversations take place. But, according to recent Barna research among youth and young adults, social media may be more of a hindrance than a help in this regard. Social media is most often about the 150 (or 220, the average number of Facebook friends, at last count[10]), not the 5 to 15.

Which is fine! Staying connected to the 150, and making new connections, is just fine—as long as it's not at the expense of the 5 to 15. Unfortunately, it appears that many people (especially teens and young adults) don't know how to put social media in its proper place in their lives.

When "likes" and comments are the relational gold standard, few can afford to invest in transformative spiritual conversations. This is where churches can help. What are some specific ways your faith community can offer biblical wisdom to people struggling with both online and real-life relationships? And, in the digital age, how can you equip people to use tech tools and online platforms wisely, to expand and enhance the meaningful relationships they are learning how to build?

NEVER LET A GOOD CONFLICT GO TO WASTE

As we've seen, fear of relational tension ranks first on the list of reasons people avoid spiritual conversations, followed closely by discomfort with how religion is politicized. And, granted, there is a lot of cultural and often personal baggage stacked against initiating conversations about faith. As Roxanne Stone wrote in the introduction, "To be against something (or *someone*) is frowned upon in America today, whether that's women's reproductive rights, same-sex marriage or the efficacy of another religion. . . . Walking the fine line between tolerance and one's convictions is a difficult challenge for many Christians."

This is where gentleness and respect must come in. As any happily married person can tell you, conflict isn't the problem; in fact, conflict is often a chance to learn more about the other person, to find out what's most important to her or him, to draw close and discover what makes them tick. Why let that opportunity go to waste?

Instead of avoiding potential conflict, how can the faith community equip Christians to draw close with gentleness and respect?

When "likes" and comments are the relational gold standard, few can afford to invest in transformative spiritual conversations

GET CONFIDENT TO SHARE BY SHARING

Many of the eager conversationalists we met through this study seem to have a positive-feedback loop of talking about their faith and confidence to talk about their faith. The more they do it, the more confident they feel about doing it. (And the more confident they feel . . . you get it.)

A church's approach to Christians' crisis of confidence is often to arm them with more information, such as training them in apologetics. This can be helpful, especially for those who are new to faith, but it doesn't appear to be a cure-all. What is essential for building confidence in faith sharing is *practice*. Like praying, sharing the good news of Christ is a skill one learns by doing.

Let's help people understand that they don't need to know everything in order to share something. "I don't know" and "Let's find out together" are both acceptable answers—even clergymembers should practice them. (Maybe even out loud.)

What Christians need to know and share is what God has done and is doing in their own life—and if they haven't thought much about this, it's no wonder they're not sharing it. Remember, the more people think about God, the more they talk about him. When nonbelievers ask about their hope, how many in your faith community are ready to give *their own* answer? How can you help them tell their own story of new life in Christ?

This is not an idle question. If redemption and restoration are *actually* available through the life, death and resurrection of Christ Jesus . . . and if the Spirit of God *actually* takes up residence in those who call Jesus Lord . . . and if, as Jesus preached, the kingdom of God is *actually* near . . . then that's worth talking about.

> What Christians need to know and share is what God has done and is doing in their own life

NOTES

1. "Is Evangelism Going Out of Style?" Barna.com, December 17, 2013. https://www.barna.com/research/is-evangelism-going-out-of-style/ (accessed February 2018).

2. David Kinnaman and Gabe Lyons, *Good Faith: Being a Christian When Society Thinks You're Irrelevant or Extreme* (Grand Rapids, MI: Baker Books, 2016), 42.

3. Barna Group, *Gen Z: The Culture, Beliefs and Motivations Shaping the Next Generation* (Ventura, CA: Barna Group, 2018), 22.

4. John Suler, "The Online Disinhibition Effect," *CyberPsychology & Behavior,* July 2004, 7(3), 321–326. https://doi.org/10.1089/1094931041291295 (accessed February 2018).

5. Matthias R. Mehl, et. al., "Eavesdropping on Happiness: Well-Being Is Related to Having Less Small Talk and More Substantive Conversations," *Psychological Science,* April 2010, 539–541. doi: 10.1177/0956797610362675 (accessed February 2018).

6. Jonathan Merritt, *Learning to Speak God from Scratch: Why Sacred Words and Vanishing— and How We Can Revive Them* (New York: Convergent Books, 2018).

7. Stephanie L. Derrick, "Christmas and Cricket: Rediscovering Two Lost C. S. Lewis Articles After 70 Years," *Christianity Today,* December 15, 2017. http://www.christianitytoday.com/ct/2017/december-web-only/christmas-cricket-lost-c-s-lewis-articles.html (accessed March 2018).

8.   Jean M. Twenge, "Have Smartphones Destroyed a Generation?" *The Atlantic Monthly,* September 2017. https://www.theatlantic.com/magazine/archive/2017/09/has-the-smart-phone-destroyed-a-generation/534198/ (accessed March 2018).

9.   Emerging Technology, "Your Brain Limits You to Just Five BFFs," *MIT Technology Review,* April 29, 2016. https://www.technologyreview.com/s/601369/your-brain-limits-you-to-just-five-bffs/ (accessed March 2018).

10. Aaron Smith, "6 New Facts About Facebook," Pew Research Center, February 3, 2014. http://www.pewresearch.org/fact-tank/2014/02/03/6-new-facts-about-facebook/ (accessed March 2018).

METHODOLOGY

IN-DEPTH SURVEY (QUALITATIVE)

An exploratory, open-ended, online survey was conducted among 102 Christians to understand more about their spiritual conversations as well as online interactions. This survey was conducted between April 20 and May 15, 2017.

NATIONALLY REPRESENTATIVE SURVEY (QUANTITATIVE)

The primary source of data in this report is a survey of 1,714 U.S. adults, comprised of an over-sample of 535 Millennials and 689 Practicing Christians, conducted online June 22–July 13, 2017. Respondents were recruited from a national consumer panel, and minimal weighting was applied to ensure representation of certain demographic factors, such as age, gender, ethnicity and region. The sample error for this data is plus or minus 2.2% at the 95% confidence level for the total sample. A subgroup of participants had either: "shared my views on faith or religion in the last 5 years" OR "someone has shared their views on faith or religion with me in the last 5 years."

DEFINITIONS

Self-identified Christians select "Christian" from a list of religious affiliations.

Non-Christians do not self-identify as Christian.

Churched Christians identify as Christian and have attended church within the past six months.

Unchurched Christians identify as Christian but have not attended church within the past six months.

Practicing Christians identify as Christian, have attended church within the past month and strongly agree that their faith is very important in their life today.

Non-practicing Christians identify as Christian, but do not qualify as practicing under the definition above.

Eager conversationalists identify as Christian and have had 10 or more conversations about faith in the past year.

Reluctant conversationalists identify as Christian and have had between zero and nine conversations about faith in the past year.

Gen Z were born 1999 to 2015 (only 13- to 18-year-olds included).
Millennials were born 1984 to 1998.
Gen X were born 1965 to 1983.
Boomers were born 1946 to 1964.
Elders were born before 1946.

ACKNOWLEDGMENTS

Barna Group wishes to thank our partners at Lutheran Hour Ministries, including and especially Ashley Bayless, Kurt Buchholz, Tony Cook and Jeff Craig-Meyer. Heartfelt thanks also to our gracious contributors to this project: Jefferson Bethke, Dana Byers, Micah Glenn and Rachel Legouté.

The research team for *Spiritual Conversations in the Digital Age* is Brooke Hempell, Susan Mettes, Roxanne Stone and Pam Jacob. Under the editorial direction of Roxanne Stone, Aly Hawkins and Susan Mettes analyzed the data and wrote this report. David Kinnaman contributed additional analysis and insights. Doug Brown edited the manuscript. Roxanne Stone developed the data visualizations, which were designed, along with the cover, by Chaz Russo. Annette Allen designed the report. Brenda Usery managed production with help from Todd White.

The research team wishes to thank our Barna colleagues Amy Brands, Bill Denzel, Cory Maxwell-Coghlan, Steve McBeth, Caitlin Schuman, Jess Villa and Alyce Youngblood.

ABOUT THE PROJECT PARTNERS

Barna Group is a research firm dedicated to providing actionable insights on faith and culture, with a particular focus on the Christian church. In its 30-year history, Barna has conducted more than one million interviews in the course of hundreds of studies, and has become a go-to source for organizations that want to better understand a complex and changing world from a faith perspective.

www.Barna.com

Barna's clients and partners include a broad range of academic institutions, churches, nonprofits and businesses, such as Alpha, the Templeton Foundation, Fuller Seminary, the Bill and Melinda Gates Foundation, Maclellan Foundation, DreamWorks Animation, Focus Features, Habitat for Humanity, The Navigators, NBC-Universal, the ONE Campaign, Paramount Pictures, the Salvation Army, Walden Media, Sony and World Vision. The firm's studies are frequently quoted by major media outlets such as *The Economist,* BBC, CNN, *USA Today,* the *Wall Street Journal,* Fox News, Huffington Post, *The New York Times* and the *Los Angeles Times.*

Lutheran Hour Ministries is a trusted expert in global media that equips and engages a vibrant volunteer base to passionately proclaim the gospel to more than 71 million people worldwide each week. Through its headquarters in St. Louis, Missouri, and ministry centers on six continents, LHM reaches into more than 50 countries, often bringing Christ to places where no other Christian evangelistic organizations are present.

www.LHM.org

Stay Informed About Cultural Trends

Barna

Barna Trends 2018
A beautifully designed and engaging look at today's trending topics that includes new data, analysis, infographics, and interviews right at your fingertips.

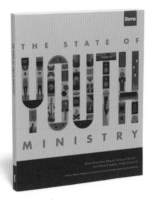

State of Youth Ministry
A wide-angle view of the youth ministry landscape that will spark conversations and lead to more effective student ministries, healthier youth workers, and sturdier teen faith.

Gen Z
Critical data to help the church effectively reach, serve and equip the emerging generation, helping them to confidently follow Jesus in today's rapidly changing culture.

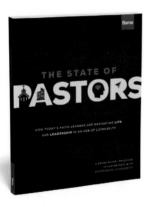

The State of Pastors
Pastoring in a complex cultural moment is not easy. Read about how church leaders are holding up in this whole-life assessment of U.S. pastors.

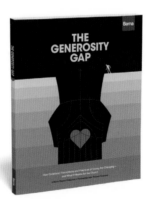

The Generosity Gap
Generosity is changing. Read about how pastors and laypeople perceive and practice generosity, and learn methods for strengthening giving habits.

The Bible in America
Analysis, insights and encouragement for those who want to understand Scripture engagement today and how to cultivate faith that lasts in an ever-changing world.